Robert E. Stevens, Ph.D., is a business marketing professor at Oral Roberts University in Tulsa, Oklahoma. In addition to membership in several prestigious business associations, he has been directly involved in executive development programs and public service activities and has written many articles and books, including *Strategic Marketing Plan Master Guide*, published by Prentice-Hall.

Formerly a business professor and administrator of the MBA Program at Oral Roberts University, **Philip K. Sherwood** is vice-president of Ruddick and Associates, a market and communications research company in Tulsa. He holds a B.A. in political science, an MBA, and a doctorate in administration.

A SPECTRUM BOOK

Prentice-Hall, Inc., Englewood Cliffs, New Jersey 07632

A Step-by-Step Guide
Including 3 Model Studies

ROBERT E. STEVENS
PHILIP K. SHERWOOD

HOW TO PREPARE A FEASIBILITY STUDY

Library of Congress Cataloging in Publication Data

Stevens, Robert E.
    How to prepare a feasibility study.

    "A Spectrum Book."
    Includes index.
    1. Cost effectiveness.   2. New products.   I. Sherwood,
Philip K.   II. Title.   III. Title.:Feasibility study: a
step-by-step guide.
HD47.4.S76   658.4'012   82-7480
ISBN 0-13-429258-8   AACR2
ISBN 0-13-429241-3 (pbk.)

This Spectrum Book is available to businesses and organizations
at a special discount when ordered in large quantities. For
information, contact Prentice-Hall, Inc., General Publishing
Division, Special Sales, Englewood Cliffs, N.J. 07632

1   2   3   4   5   6   7   8   9   10

Editorial/production supervision
and interior design by Kimberly Mazur
Cover design by Jeannette Jacobs
Manufacturing buyer: Barbara A. Frick

ISBN 0-13-429258-8

ISBN 0-13-429241-3 {PBK.}

Prentice-Hall International, Inc., *London*
Prentice-Hall of Australia Pty. Limited, *Sydney*
Prentice-Hall Canada Inc., *Toronto*
Prentice-Hall of India Private Limited, *New Delhi*
Prentice-Hall of Japan, Inc., *Tokyo*
Prentice-Hall of Southeast Asia Pte. Ltd., *Singapore*
Whitehall Books Limited, *Wellington, New Zealand*

CONTENTS

PREFACE

The purpose of this book is twofold: (1) to provide those who have an opportunity or a responsibility to prepare a feasibility study with an understanding of the concepts and procedures used in feasibility analysis so that the study can be carried out in a systematic way, and (2) to provide those who must evaluate a feasibility study with sufficient background on the topic to critically analyze the work of others who have prepared such a study.

The authors have had considerable experience in preparing feasibility studies but have been unable to find a comprehensive description of exactly what should be contained in a feasibility study or what the end results should look like. The book offers a step-by-step approach to the feasibility study along with an appendix on source of data and another containing three feasibility studies prepared by the authors.

The five chapters in the book were written with two basic criteria in mind: (1) a comprehensive coverage of concepts and procedures, and (2) a writing style practically oriented with high readability. Although this book is intended primarily for the business practitioner, it could also be used as a supplemental text for undergraduate or graduate business courses in which some attention is devoted to feasibility analysis.

Special thanks go to Jane Olsen and Eklaine Drain, who typed the manuscripts for this book. Also to John Blaho and Nancy Sailor, who aided in preparing the appendixes.

Special thanks are due to Dr. Thomas T. Ivy, Dr. Carle M. Hunt, and Dr. R. Henry Migliore, for their help in preparing some of the material included in the appendixes. All errors of commission or omission remain those of the authors.

This book is dedicated to our wives and children:

Elizabeth Ann, Robby, Richy, Jim, Beth, Joel, John, and Mark Stevens.

Jean, Scott, Jeana, and Sarah Sherwood.

INTRODUCTION
TO
FEASIBILITY
ANALYSIS

To analyze the feasibility of any undertaking in a business context is to ask one basic question: "Will the returns from the operation be sufficient to justify the investment of funds needed to carry out the operation?" For the profit-oriented organization this means a sufficient level of profits, and for the nonprofit organization this means at least covering costs.

The basic purpose of a feasibility study is to analyze this question *before* a decision is made to undertake some endeavor. This statement appears so simple that making it seems to state only the obvious. However, a moment's reflection on the number of products and retail, manufacturing, and nonprofit organizations that fail each year provides evidence that either the question of feasibility was never asked or a poor answer was provided. Although a feasibility study cannot assure the success of a venture, it should help reduce the uncertainties of a decision-making situation about a proposed venture. For many undertakings, no formal feasibility analysis is undertaken prior to the decision to undertake a project. This practice often results in failures that could have been eliminated with proper feasibility analysis.

TYPES OF FEASIBILITY STUDIES

There are many situations in which a formal feasibility study should be prepared before making a decision. For purposes of illustration, we use the introduction of a new product to show how feasibility studies fit into a decision-making process.

Before a product is introduced onto the market, a series of steps should be taken to establish a sound basis for new product development. At least six steps have been identified that should precede product introduction:

1. Idea generation
2. Feasibility analysis
3. Product development
4. Placement testing
5. Test marketing
6. Commercialization

The completion of each of these steps can be viewed as a "go-no go" decision. In other words, Step 2 is not undertaken unless the idea is evaluated as viable; Step 3 is not undertaken unless the results of the feasibility analysis are positive, and so on. This approach is used because the completion of each step involves a larger commitment of company resources and because it helps avoid putting ill-conceived products on the market before collecting sufficient evidence to warrant their introduction onto the market.

Although the sequence of steps, the nature of the data, and the magnitude of the decision differ from situation to situation, there are several identifiable decisions that should be preceded by a formal feasibility study. Some of the typical decision-making situations are as follows:

1. Introducing a new product
2. Starting a new business
3. Adding a branch facility
4. Offering new services that involve additional investment

Thus retailers, manufacturers, wholesalers, bankers, nonprofit institutions, and potential investors all face some decision-making situations that would justify a feasibility study because each of the four situations identified in the foregoing list involves analyzing potential returns from an investment.

Feasibility Study Format

Regardless of whichever of the decision-making situations is involved, a feasibility study should contain at least three basic types of analysis: (1) demand analysis, (2) costs analysis, and (3) analysis of return on investment or breakeven. Appendix B contains three separate feasibility studies that illustrate different types of situations, each following this format.

One of the most beneficial ways of combining these three analyses is to embrace the concept of a pro forma income statement (see Table 1-1) as the basic document to be generated from the feasibility study. A pro forma income statement is a projected income statement for a specific future time period using estimates of revenues and costs within that time period. It provides an estimate of cash flows to be produced by a given venture that can be discounted to determine the present value of a stream of income from the project. This estimate is used in calculating the anticipated rate of return for the venture or breakeven for nonprofit ventures.

TABLE 1-1. Pro Forma Income Statement

	Low (Pessimistic)	Medium (Most Likely)	High (Optimistic)
Sales	$3,500,000	$4,500,000	$5,500,000
Cost of Sales	2,500,000	3,400,000	4,300,000
Gross Margin	$1,000,000	$1,100,000	$1,200,000
Expenses			
Direct Selling	457,000	480,000	512,000
Advertising	157,000	168,000	180,000
Transportation and Storage	28,000	38,000	48,000
Depreciation	15,000	15,000	15,000
Credit and Collections	12,000	14,000	16,000
Financial and Clerical	29,000	38,000	47,000
Administrative	55,000	55,000	55,000
Total Expenses	$ 753,000	$ 808,000	$ 873,000
Profit Before Taxes	$ 247,000	$ 292,000	$ 327,000
Net Profit After Taxes	$ 128,440	$ 151,840	$ 170,040
Cash Flow	$ 143,440	$ 166,840	$ 185,040

Profit-oriented Feasibility Analysis

The approach for a proposed new product shown in Table 1-1 consists of the development of three alternate pro formas based on different assumptions of demand for the new product. This design permits identifying the most optimistic, most pessimistic, and the most likely outcome. It is also in line with a more realistic approach to demand forecasting for producing a range of sales volume for new projects. When products or services have already been on the market for several years, an industry sales history is available to project sales.

Revenues and costs change over the course of a product's life cycle. High investments in promotion and building distribution produce losses in early years. Increased production efficiency, technological improvement, and reduced variable costs may produce high profit levels in later years.

Because the feasibility study usually covers several years, either an annual pro forma must be estimated for an assumed project life, or an "average" year three to five years into the future can be used. Then the discounted cash flows from this year are used as an average for the venture's anticipated life to calculate the return on investment (ROI) or breakeven point.

If subjective probabilities were assigned to each alternative, then decision tree analysis could be used to calculate an expected value for the cash flow from the project. Otherwise the ROI could be calculated for each alternative and compared with a predetermined rate to evaluate the financial impact.

Developing a pro forma income statement requires forecasts of sales and operating expenses. The procedures for developing these estimates are discussed in later chapters.

From the preceding discussion we can see that the demand analysis produces an estimate of revenues, the costs analysis produces an estimate of the costs associated with those revenues, and the analysis of ROI or breakeven relates those returns to the investment to be made in the decision. This information answers the basic question analyzed in feasibility studies: Does the return from an operation justify the investment of funds?

Nonprofit Feasibility Analysis

There are many nonprofit organizations that fail to apply this basic approach to decision making. A large hospital, for example, decided to build a new wing for geriatric outpatients for rehabilitation services to patients suffering from such major trauma as stroke or heart attack. The facility was built to accommodate 100 patients. It opened and only two patients showed up to take advantage of the new facility. An analysis of demand for such services prior to building the facility would have avoided such a costly mistake.

Although the analysis of returns from a decision for a nonprofit organization are evaluated with different criteria, they should be evaluated nonetheless. Feasibility analysis is simply an application of a basic management concept: Evaluate the impact of a decision *before* you make it. This principle applies to nonprofit as well as to profit-oriented institutions.

SUMMARY

The feasibility study is a study of impacts—revenues, costs, and returns—of a decision. Formal feasibility analysis should precede major decisions that can dramatically affect a firm's financial position for years. Call it feasibility analysis, cost-benefit analysis, or whatever, the approach described in this book has application to a large number of decision-making situations.

Chapter 2 focuses on demand analysis, Chapter 3 on costs analysis, Chapter 4 on analysis of returns, and Chapter 5 on putting together the final report.

DEMAND
ANALYSIS

Analysis of demand consists of four steps: identifying a market, identifying market factors, estimating market potential, and estimating the revenues anticipated from a given venture. This chapter examines each of these steps.

IDENTIFYING A MARKET

One fundamental concept that underlies demand analysis is that a market for a product or service is actually a composite of smaller markets, each with identifiable characteristics. When we speak of the automobile market, we are referring to a large market composed of smaller submarkets or segments. This market can be segmented in several ways to identify the various submarkets. The size of the car different consumers want, for example, could be used to identify at least four submarkets or segments: full size, intermediate, compact, and subcompact. This process of breaking up a market into its constituent parts is usually called market segmentation. The basic premise is that the consumers in one market are different from the consumers in another market, and each group represents a separate entity.

The rationale for market segmentation is the reality that markets are too complex and diverse to consider all consumers within the market as homogeneous. If a new product or service is to appeal to teenagers, for example, then that segment or part of the total market between the ages of thirteen to nineteen is the market of interest. Only its size and characteristics must be identified and studied and not those of the other segments which are not included.

Bases for Market Segmentation

Several bases are commonly used for segmentation.[1] These include: geographic, demographic, product usage, and product benefits. A discussion of the use of market grids is also presented in this section to show how several of the bases can be combined for analysis and construction of individual market segments.

Geographic and Demographic Segmentation. The most commonly used bases for segmentation use geographic and demographic variables to segment markets. Geographic segmentation

[1]The bases are discussed in detail in David L. Kurtz and Louis E. Boone's *Marketing,* the Dryden Press, Hinsdale, Ill., 1981, pp. 152–160.

uses census tracks, cities, trade areas, counties, states, regions, or countries as the basis of segmentation. For many products, this is a logical framework. Snowmobiles, for example, are going to be purchased only in areas with sufficient snowfall. These areas can be geographically identified as one basis for segmentation.

Demographic segmentation involves using variables such as sex, age, income, educational level, and so on as the basis for segmenting a market. In the market grids used in the following section, age and sex are used as two variables to segment the clothing market. These variables are appropriate for many products and services.

Geographic and demographic characteristics of industrial consumers can also be useful in segmenting industrial markets. In fact, some customers are concentrated both geographically and by industry in certain industrial markets. Tire manufacturers in Ohio and the electronics manufacturers in California are two examples of geographical and industry concentration.

Segmentation by Product Usage. A recent approach to market segmentation uses the product usage patterns of consumers as the basis for segmentation. Consumers are classified as users or nonusers, and users are further classified as light, medium, and heavy users. In some product categories a small percentage of the consumers account for a majority of the purchasers. Air travel, car rental, dog food, and hair coloring are such products. Usage rates can become an important market segmentation base.

Benefit Segmentation. Another way to segment markets is by the benefits the buyers expect from purchase or use of a product. In one study, the toothpaste market was segmented on such bases as flavor and product appearance, brightness of teeth, decay prevention, and price. Each of these variables represents the principal benefits sought by the purchaser. Each of these benefit segments is composed of consumers with different demographics, personalities, life-styles, and so on. Each represents a distinct market segment.

Market Grids

One basic tool that can be used to segment a market is a *market grid*.[2] A market grid is a two dimensional view of a market that is

[2]For more discussion of this type of analysis see E. Jerome McCarthy's *Basic Marketing: A Managerial Approach*, Richard D. Irwin, Inc., Homewood, Ill., 1981, Chapter 9.

divided into various segments using characteristics of potential customers. There are two important concepts in grid analysis. First, characteristics of potential consumers rather than product characteristics are used to segment the market to insure a market-oriented view instead of a product-oriented view of the market. Second, the important characteristics to focus upon are those of the potential consumers not currently being served by the firm rather than those of existing consumers.

Normally a series of grids must be used to completely describe a market, so one must begin with a set of characteristics thought to be useful in differentiating consumers. Each characteristic must be analyzed to determine its probable effect on a market.

The characteristics normally include geographic, socioeconomic, behavioral, and/or psychological dimensions. The objective is to isolate a specific market rather than a general market. Most products or services are not consumed by everyone, so those people or companies which are most likely to consume an offering must be identified.

Once a list of potential consumer characteristics has been developed, the next step is actual grid construction. Figures 2-1 and 2-2 show two grids for clothing. Each section within the grid is actually a market segment for clothing. Notice that as each characteristic is used to identify a specific segment it becomes possible to begin to describe a market permitting collection of data on that specific market. These grids illustrate the breakdown approach to market segmentation where the total market is broken up into various submarkets.

The two shaded areas in the first grid (Figure 2-1) represent two completely different market segments. The styles of clothes

FIGURE 2-1. Grid 1 for Clothing

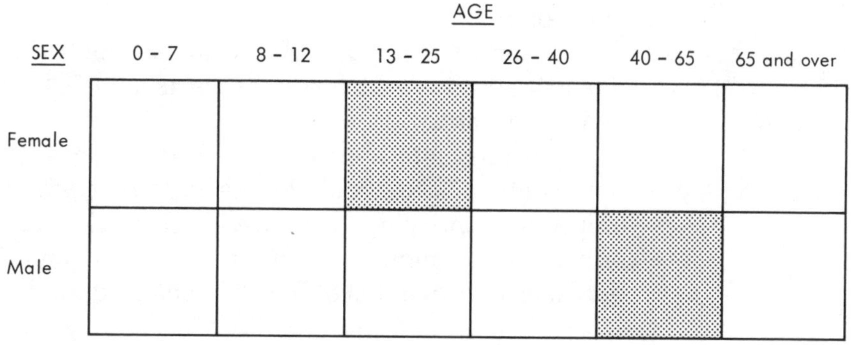

needed, the emphasis on styles, the types of stores these consumers would prefer to shop at, buying motives, all of these would normally be quite different and represent different markets.

INCOME

ACTIVITY	Lower	Middle	Upper
Leisure			
Formal			
Work	▒▒▒▒		▒▒▒▒
Recreation & Sporting			

FIGURE 2-2. Grid 2 for Clothing

Upon examining the two shaded areas in the second grid (Figure 2-2) it also becomes apparent that the consumers represent different market segments. You wouldn't expect a sanitation worker and a bank president to need the same types of clothes for work; therefore, they may not shop at the same retail outlets. As a market segment emerges through the analysis, it represents a potential group of consumers with similar characteristics that define a market. For smaller companies only one or a few segments may be of interest. A large firm may select several segments as potential target markets because they plan to develop, or have already developed, a complete line of products or services. Whether one or many segments are selected, this type of analysis is needed.

Some of the types of characteristics for consumer and industrial markets which may serve as a basis for segmentation are shown in Table 2-1.

An alternate approach to developing a grid or diagram to represent a market would be the *buildup approach*. This approach involves identifying the individual market segments and then putting the segments together to represent a market. The result is the same: a recognition of the different needs of different consumers.

14

TABLE 2–1. Consumer Characteristics by Consumer Type

| Characteristics | CONSUMER TYPE | |
	Ultimate Consumers	Industrial
Socioeconomic	Age	Size—volume
	Sex	Number of employees
	Income	Number of plants
	Education	Types of organization
	Marital status	Industry
Behavioral*	Brands purchased	Decision makers
	Coupon redemption	Growth markets
	Stores shopped	Public vs. private
	Loyalty	Distribution pattern
	Hobbies	
	Reading interest	
Psychological*	Attitudes	Management attitudes
	Personality traits	Management awareness
	Awareness	Management style
	Recall	

aThese would include psychographic characteristics.

An example of this approach for an industrial product is shown in Figure 2-3. This is a reconstruction of the market for component parts of mud pumps used on oil rigs. In conducting the consumer analysis, it was found that the market was dominated

FIGURE 2-3. OEM Market for Mud Pump Components

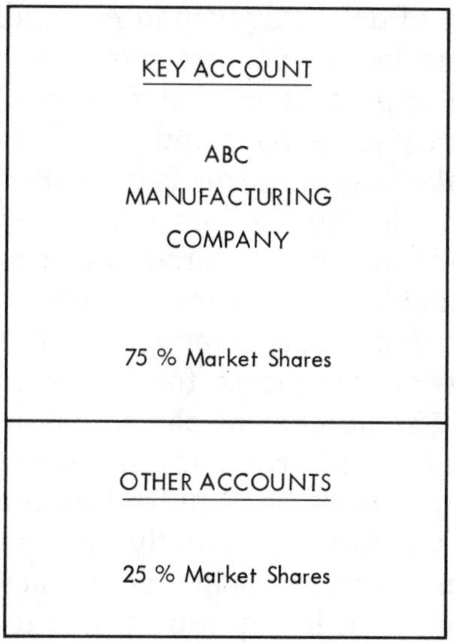

KEY ACCOUNT

ABC
MANUFACTURING
COMPANY

75 % Market Shares

OTHER ACCOUNTS

25 % Market Shares

by one firm. This firm accounted for about 75% of the original equipment manufacturer (OEM) sales in this market with the remaining 25% of the sales volume divided among four other firms. The large manufacturer was designated a key account, meaning it was considered as a distinct segment of the market.

MARKET FACTORS

Market factors are those realities in the market which cause the demand for the product. For example, the market factor for baby beds is the number of babies born each year. Since a market is merely people with money and a motivation to buy, population figures and income figures are commonly used as market factors. However, it is usually possible to be much more specific in identifying market factors for a given company, product, or service. The interest in identifying market factors is threefold: to identify the factors that influence the demand for the product or service; to determine the relationship between the factor and the product or service; and to forecast that market factor for future years. Since many of the same market factors are used by different forecasters, much of the forecasting work may have already been completed and simply needs to be located. Population projections, for example, are available through many sources, so there is usually no need to develop your own population forecast. Potential sources of data are given in Appendix A.

Two basic techniques are available for selecting and determining the impact of market factors on a given product or service: *arbitrary judgement* and *correlation analysis*. Arbitrary judgement makes use of the decision maker's own experience and judgement in selecting factors and weighing them. This is a common technique for new products or services since no sales history is available unless a test market is used. For example, a drug manufacturer might determine from historical data that $2 worth of drugs are purchased for each person residing in a given market area. The number of consumers in a market area is the market factor for that product, and projection of population for that market area would be used for information of its future size.

A more complex, yet usually more reliable, approach is to use correlation analysis to help identify factors and assign weights to them. Although it is not appropriate to discuss the details of this technique here, there is a specific technique in correlation analysis called *step-wise regression analysis* that not only weights the various factors, but also provides a measure of what the addition of each factor gives to an explanation of changes in sales. This method requires a sales history, so it is limited mainly to existing products or new products for which test market data is available.

Regardless of the technique used in analyzing market factors, the basic information sought deals with understanding the factors influencing demand for a produce or service and the historical and future trends of those factors. The use of market factors to estimate market potential will be discussed in the next section.

MARKET POTENTIAL

Once a market has been divided into various segments, and the characteristics of consumers and market factors in each market has been analyzed, the next step is to estimate the size of the market. The term *market potential* is used to refer to the expected sales of a product or service for an entire market. More simply, 'If everybody that could buy would buy, how many units or dollars worth of sales would occur?" The answer to that question is the market potential. A market segment which does not have enough consumers spending enough dollars does not justify effort in that market unless a firm is seeking to accomplish some nonrevenue objective. You are not just seeking consumer markets but markets which can be served profitably by the firm attempting to meet their needs. Market potential is a quantitative measure of a market's capacity to consume a product in a given time period. This measure is a prerequisite to assessing profitability.

Estimating Potential for Existing Products. Market potential can be measured either in absolute or relative terms. An *absolute measure* is one which is expressed in units or dollars, whereas a *relative measure* relates one part of a market to another and is expressed as a percent. We will discuss one technique for estimating relative potential and two techniques for estimating absolute measures of potential. These techniques are used when products and services are already on the market and the future size of the market is desired.

The Sales Index Measure
of Relative Potential

The *sales index method* provides a relative measure of potential for products which have reached the maturity stage of their product life cycle. This technique is useful in answering questions about the relative potential of various geographical market areas. Its use requires familiarity with the product's stage in its life cycle, penetration of distribution in various areas, and a sales history.[3]

This technique is illustrated in Table 2-2. Notice that the resulting figures are percentages of total industry sales by region. This shows that industry sales will occur next year in the same proportion as last year's in each region. The potential in the northwest region is expected to be 23.2% of the total—whatever that total turns out to be next year. One region can be compared to another using this measure of potential.

TABLE 2-2. Sales Index Method*

Region	Industry Sales	Sales Index	Potential
Northeast	$ 8,500,009	28.8%	28.8%
Southeast	6,753,090	22.8	22.8
Northwest	6,870,421	23.2	23.2
Southwest	7,430,218	25.2	25.2
	$29,553,738	100.0%	100.0%

*Source: Artificial data

The Market Factor Method

Normally, relative potential is not adequate, and an absolute measure of potential is needed to provide estimates of potential in units or dollars. One technique used to accomplish this is the *market factor method*. This involves identifying the factors which influence a good or service's sales and relating the factors to sales in some way. This was mentioned in Chapter 1. An example of this method is shown in Table 2-3 in which population is used as the market factor. Population, the market factor, is related to sales in this example through the sales rate or dollars of sales per thousand people. Notice that absolute and relative potential could be calculated by region using the projected regional population as

[3]See Bertram Schoner and Kenneth P. Uhl's *Marketing Research Information Systems and Decision Making*, John Wiley and Sons, Inc., New York, 1975, Chapter 15, for a more detailed discussion of this technique.

the factor and the regional sales rate to relate sales to the market factor.

It should be apparent that given a market segment, the number of people in that segment, and an expenditure rate, the potential of that segment can be calculated. Using this technique produces an estimate of the absolute potential of a given market. This technique would be appropriate when an established market is being evaluated.

TABLE 2-3. The Market Factor Method

Region	Sales ($) 1980	Population (thousands)	Sales Rate (thousands)
Northeast	$ 8,500,009	68,570	$123.96
Southeast	6,753,090	38,720	174.40
Northwest	6,870,421	32,810	209.40
Southwest	7,430,218	66,730	111.34
	$29,553,738	206,830	$154.78 average

Population projection (1985) = 210,847,000
Sales rate (average) = $154.78/1000
Potential (154.78 × 210,847) = $32,633,844

The Regression Analysis Method

Another technique used to estimate potential involves the use of a statistical technique known as regression analysis. This technique still makes use of market factors but the market factors are related to sales in a more mathematically complex manner. Space does not permit a complete explanation of this technique. The purpose here is to show how it could be used in estimating potential. One result of regression analysis is an equation which relates the market factor to sales. If more than one market factor is used, then multiple regression analysis is needed. Table 2-4 shows data which has been analyzed using two market factors. The resulting equation is then used to estimate potential. The approach still requires estimates of the two market factors (independent variables) for the future period for which the measure of potential is desired. In this example, Y represents total industry sales while X_1 and X_2 represent two market factors which are related to total industry sales. Estimates of the value of these factors for the next time period are substituted into the equation to calculate an estimate of industry potential. This technique also permits calculation of a confidence interval for the estimate.

TABLE 2-4. Using Multiple Regression Analysis in Estimating Market Potential (in thousands)

Year	INDUSTRY SALES		
	Y	X_1	X_2
1968	6,860	1,329	40
1969	6,520	1,116	39
1970	6,345	1,041	40
1971	6,710	1,209	37
1972	7,222	1,553	44
1973	6,810	1,296	45
1974	7,005	1,365	44
1975	7,275	1,492	50
1976	7,450	1,641	53
1977	7,250	1,591	59
1978	7,105	1,510	66
1979	6,666	1,196	71
1980	6,900	1,322	72

$Y = a + b_1 X_1 + b_2 X_2$ general equation
$Y = 4641 + (1.70)(1600) + (-0.45)(60)$
$Y = 7,333.4$
Using this technique, the estimated market
potential for this product, Y, is 7,333.4

Estimating Potential for New Products or Services

When innovative new products or services are proposed, no industry sales figure is available as a point of reference for estimating potential. Under such circumstances, it is still important to identify market factors that are likely to influence the demand for the product or service. These factors can provide an upper limit to demand. Knowing that there were five million men in a particular income and age category would be a useful reference point in beginning an analysis of potential for a new product for males with these two characteristics. However, you would not expect all of the five million men to buy the product. Three techniques commonly used to refine estimates of potential from that upper limit are judgemental estimates, consumer surveys, and the substitute method.

Judgemental Estimates. Judgment involves use of expert opinion of those knowledgeable about the market and product. This judgement can be used in a formalized approach such as the

Delphi technique, or it can involve pooled estimates and a reconciliation of difference between estimates given by different people.

Consumer Surveys.   Surveys of potential consumers can be used to estimate potential new products. This approach is especially useful for industrial products where the number of consumers is smaller and they can be more readily identified. For example, a part used in mud pumps for oil drilling rigs would have a small, easily identifiable market of a few customers—manufacturers of mud pumps—whose potential purchases of the part can be estimated. The more diverse consumer market makes this technique more difficult to use, but it can be adapted to consumer goods.

Substitute Method.   Most new products are substitutes for existing products on the market. If the size of these markets can be estimated, then the sales of the new product can be estimated based on the replacement potential for existing products. An acceptance rate would have to be estimated for the proportion of existing consumers who would switch to the new product when it was introduced on the market. This acceptance rate could be estimated through consumer research.

Forecasting Sales

After the size of the total market has been estimated, the next step is to estimate the expected annual sales revenue generated by the proposed project. This is not trying to determine how many consumers will buy a product or service, but how many will buy *your* product or service.

For established markets, this means estimating market share. The question to be answered is: "What share of total sales can we reasonably expect to attain?" The percent is then converted to a dollar amount which is the sales revenue portion of the pro forma income statement. The key element in the estimate at this point is judgement. If a test market is used later in the development process, this estimate can be reevaluated as to soundness.

This judgement is based on an analysis of your offering, versus competitive offerings. If four competitors were already in the market and your product—the fifth one—was expected to compete on an equal footing with other offerings, then a 20% market share would be used as an initial estimate of market share.

This basic estimate would then be raised or lowered to reflect competitive strengths and weaknesses in the market. Regression analysis is also commonly used in forecasting for products already on the market.

For new products and services not currently on the market, an *acceptance rate* or *penetration rate* must be estimated. The acceptance rate is the proportion of the segment which will buy your product or use your service. Two approaches can be used to estimate the acceptance rate. These are described below.

Judgement Estimates. One way to estimate the acceptance rate is to use judgement. After careful analysis of the market, the person preparing the feasibility study together with other people who are knowledgable about the market, sets the rate. This in effect is an "educated guess" but can be effective if people who are knowledgable about a market, such as retailers, wholesalers, industrial users, and the like are consulted. This estimate also reflects what the company could bring to the market in terms of marketing skills and innovation, and so on.

Consumer Surveys. Another approach to estimating the proportion of consumers who would buy a new offering is a survey of consumers. This has been referred to as "iffy" data: "I would buy your product *if* it were offered on the market and *if* I was in market at that time, and *if*. . . ."

The consumer survey approach can be highly effective for industrial users since they are in a position to evaluate the use of a product in a more judicious manner than many individual consumers.

The judgement estimate and consumer survey approaches are often combined to provide a sales forecast. A set of assumptions must also be developed as a basis for the forecast. Assumptions about market acceptance, competitive reactions, economic conditions, and the like must precede the actual dollar forecast used in the pro forma income statement.

An example of how these approaches can be combined to estimate sales revenue is shown in Table 2-5. It shows the estimates of attendance to a proposed water-recreation center. Assumptions are made about the penetration or acceptance rates by market segment and repeat visits.

TABLE 2.5. Attendance Projections

	ATTENDANCE ALTERNATIVE 1980 FORECASTS		
	---	---	---
Facts and Assumptions	Low	Most Likely	High
Local Market—Target Population			
Target Market (Ages 10–25)	112,000	112,000	112,000
Penetration	.65	.70	.85
Attendance	72,800	78,400	95,200
Local Market—General Population			
Population	103,087	103,087	103,087
Penetration	.03	.05	.07
Attendance	3,100	5,100	7,200
Regional Market			
Population	90,000	90,000	90,000
Penetration	.10	.15	.20
Attendance	9,000	13,500	18,000
Tourist Market			
Population	225,000	225,000	225,000
Penetration	.03	.05	.07
Attendance	6,750	11,250	15,750
Group Sales Market			
Attendance	18,275	20,350	25,700
Repeat Business			
Attendance	72,800	78,400	95,200
TOTAL ATTENDANCE	182,725	207,000	257,050

The admission charge was anticipated to be $5,000 per person, giving the following alternative sales forecasts:

Low Forecast	$ 913,625 (182,725 × $5)
Most Likely	$1,035,000 (207,000 × $5)
High Forecast	$1,285,250 (257,050 × $5)

A sales range of about $900,000 to $1,300,000 was estimated. To derive a figure for the pro forma income statement, the following probabilities were assigned to each forecast:

FORECAST LEVEL/PROBABILITY ASSIGNED

Low Forecast	0.25
Most Likely	0.50
High Forecast	0.25

The expected sales revenue was then computed as follows:

$$E_{SR} = (\$913,625)\,(.25) + (\$1,035,000)\,(.50) + (\$1,285,250)\,(.25)$$

$$E_{SR} = \$1,067,218.$$

This final value (\$1,067,218) was used as the estimated sales revenue to be generated from attendance sales in the pro forma income statement.

SUMMARY

Although estimating potential revenues is extremely difficult, it must be done. The estimate of revenues is used as the sales figure for the pro forma income statement. A detailed example of how sales revenues are estimated using secondary sources of data plus promoter inputs from consumers is given in Appendix B, in the feasibility study for the Blueridge Packing Company.

Chapter 3 discusses procedures for projecting costs to complete the pro forma income statement.

COST
ANALYSIS

The bottom line of any operation or project is significantly affected by the underlying cost structure. Consequently, cost analysis is closely allied with demand analysis as discussed in Chapter 2. Once the process of demand analysis is accomplished by identifying the market, identifying market factors, estimating market potential, and estimating the revenues anticipated from a given venture, cost analysis must be carefully considered. This chapter discusses various cost concepts; cost information sources; cost sensitivity analysis; risk analysis and cost forecasting, including technical analysis; and forecasting procedures.

COST CONCEPTS

Cost analysis is a complex process used to account for costs in conducting business operations. This is also true of analyzing cost for feasibility study purposes. As a business functions, assets lose their original identity. The business operation converts the assets into some other form. For example, raw materials of many kinds may go into a final manufactured product. Many of these raw materials may be unrecognizable in the end product. However, costs are traced through the business operations as the assets and resources are converted into goods and services. Since the profits and losses of a business are measured as the difference between the revenue received from customers and the costs associated with the delivery of the products or services, a project cannot be judged as feasible or profitable without dependable cost estimates.

TYPES OF COSTS

There are many different types of costs. Consequently, costs must be selectively chosen to match the purpose for which they are used. Care must be taken to understand the specific application of a cost under consideration.

Costs can be divided into several major categories. Some of these costs will be instrumental in developing the project cost summary discussed later in the chapter.

Period Costs. Period costs are associated with and measured by time intervals rather than goods or services. For example, equipment rental may be at the rate of $1,200 per month. Regardless of the amount of business or product supported by the equipment, the rental cost of the equipment remains $1,200 per month. This expense amount is allocated against revenue according to the time interval without regard to the amount of business transacted. Equipment expense for one year will show a cost of $14,400 on the income statement. Generally speaking, selling and administrative costs are designated as period costs.

Product Costs.   In some cases it is inappropriate to classify costs as period costs. Some situations in the income determination process call for costs to be offset as expenses against the activity, good, or service that produced the revenue. Under this concept of income determination, the period in which the benefit is received is the period in which the costs should be expressed and deducted as expenses. Following our equipment rental example, the equipment rental for a certain period should not be charged off as rent expense for that period if the goods produced by the equipment are not sold until a later period. If costs of this type are handled as product costs, they are matched against the revenue generated from sales of that product during the period of that sale. In most cases, manufacturing costs are treated as product costs rather than period costs and are included in the cost of goods sold.

Fixed Costs.   Those costs which can be expected to remain constant over a period of time regardless of activity levels are called *fixed costs*. Examples of this type of cost are executive salaries, interest charges, rent, insurance, equipment leases, depreciation, engineering and technical support, and product development expense. Obviously a fixed cost can be increased or decreased like any other cost, particularly in an inflationary period. However, these variations are caused by other external factors and not by the firm's output or activity.

Fixed costs can be broken down further as *committed fixed cost* and *discretionary fixed costs*. Various management decisions will commit the company to a course of action that will require the company to conform to a certain payment schedule for a number of years in the future. These costs are committed fixed costs. The costs related to acquiring a new building are examples of committed costs. On the other hand, discretionary fixed costs are established as a part of a budget that can be altered by management action on a monthly, quarterly, or yearly basis. These costs are much more easily altered and have a high degree of flexibility. Examples of discretionary fixed costs are the research and development budget or supervisory salaries that are set by management action.

Variable and Semivariable Costs.   The costs that vary closely with production are considered to be *variable costs*. In the strictest sense of the term, variable costs should vary in direct proportion to changes in production levels. Direct material cost and direct labor costs are good examples of variable costs. However, most costs are *semivariable*. Semivariable costs tend to fluctuate with volume, but not in a direct relationship to production. Market research expense, advanced research expense, advertising and sales promotion expense, supplies expense, and maintenance expenses are all examples of semivariable expenses. In some cases semivariable costs can be broken down into fixed and variable components to make application for decision making possible.

Direct and Indirect Costs.   *Direct costs* are those identifiable with a particular product, department or activity. *Indirect costs* are not directly identifiable with any particular product, activity, or department. Often the distinction between direct and indirect costs depends upon the unit under consideration. A cost of specific supplies used may be identified directly as a cost of a particular department but not be a direct cost of the product manufactured. When a cost can be directly identified to the unit under consideration, it is considered a direct cost relative to that unit. When a cost is associated with a unit only through allocation, it is an indirect cost.

Controllable and Noncontrollable Costs.   As with direct and indirect costs, a reference point is required to classify costs as controllable or noncontrollable. Obviously at some point in the organizational structure all costs are controllable. Top management can dispose of property, eliminate personnel, terminate research projects, or do whatever is necessary to control costs. However, at middle and lower levels of management, costs can be termed as uncontrollable. If a specific level of management has the authority to authorize certain costs, then these costs are considered controllable at that level. A plant manager may have control over the supplies used by his plant, but he may have no control of promotional costs established by central headquarters.

Sunk Costs. A sunk cost is usually a cost that was spent in the past and is irrelevant to a decision under consideration. This concept will be discussed further in the next chapter in regard to the capital budgeting decision. Sunk costs may be variable or fixed.

Differential Costs. The purpose of cost analysis is to provide management with the data necessary to compare alternatives and make a choice. In order to simplify the comparison of alternatives, any costs that remain the same regardless of the alternative will be disregarded in the analysis. A difference in cost between one course of action and another is referred to as a *differential cost*. In most cases the decision will result in an increased cost. This increased differential cost is often specifically referred to as an *incremental cost*.

Differential costs are often referred to as marginal costs when the differential cost is the additional cost required to produce one more unit of a product.

Opportunity Costs. One ordinarily views costs as being outlays or expenditures that must be made to obtain goods and services. The concept of *opportunity costs* extends to include sacrifices that are made by foregoing benefits or returns. Opportunity cost takes into consideration the fact that choosing one of several alternatives precludes the receiving of the benefits of the rejected alternatives. The sacrifice of a return from a rejected alternative is referred to as the opportunity cost of the chosen alternative.

Many of the types of costs mentioned above are overlapping in nature. A fixed cost may also be a sunk cost, an uncontrollable cost or a period cost. Judgment must be used in identifying specific costs in the development of cost estimates for determining feasibility.

Data Sources

Many sources of data are found in the historical records of a company. These records can provide cost information to establish reasonable cost estimates. There are many other sources of data that provide information to form the basis of a reliable cost forecast. Some of these are listed below.

- *Trade Publications.* Provide comparative financial ratios, cost of goods sold information, gross margin data, and other information.
- *Time Studies.* Establish standards for estimating labor cost.
- *Experiments.* Test processes in terms of time, material, labor, and other resources necessary to accomplish a given activity.
- *Pilot Plant or Process Activities.* Involves the intermittent or continuous operation of a new plant activity or process to perfect engineering specifications and to establish cost standards.
- *Historical Cost Data.* Can include past material cost, labor cost, overhead expense, administrative costs, utility expense, and many other categories of expense.
- *Interviews.* Includes personal interviews, telephone interviews, and mail interviews designed to gather data that provide primary cost information unavailable from other sources.
- *Wholesale Prices and Price Indexes,* Washington, D.C.: U.S. Bureau of Labor Statistics. Provides statistical representation of various prices periodically.
- *Standard & Poor's Industry Surveys,* New York: McGraw-Hill, Inc. Provides overall statistical data and outlook for various industries. Also provides special indepth coverage in reports of specific areas such as the recreation industry, entertainment industry, and so on.
- *Agricultural Statistics,* U.S. Department of Agriculture, Washington, D.C.: U.S. Government Printing Office. Includes statistical data concerning prices and supply of agriculturally related items.
- Various *Census Reports.* Provides available information for various types of activities such as construction, wholesale trade, housing, manufacturing and transportation.
- *Department of Commerce.* Provides a large amount of resource information in the resource libraries and extensive stores of the regional offices of the Department of Commerce for forecasting purposts.
- *Business Periodical Index,* New York: H.W. Wilson, Co. Indexes areas of business interest by author and subject. Available in most libraries.
- *Thomas Register,* New York: Thomas Publishing Co. Includes products and services, company addresses, and company personnel.
- *Survey of Buying Power,* New York: Sales Management. Provides data such as population figures, income figures, and retail sales figures for specific areas of the country.
- Appendix A, Sources of Published Data. Provides further sources of information.

COST SENSITIVITY ANALYSIS

Before moving on to the actual development of detailed cost forecasts, a discussion of sensitivity analysis is in order. *Sensitivity analysis* is a technique that can illustrate how the costs of an operation or activity will be affected by changes in variables or by errors in the input data. Sensitivity analysis is sometimes called "what if" analysis, because it asks and answers questions such as: "What if labor cost increases an average of $1.75/hour?" or "What if sales fall to 350,000 units?" The starting point for sensitivity analysis is to establish a base case or most likely situation. Once the base case or most likely forecast elements are established for items like unit sales, sale price, fixed and variable costs, the analyst will selectively change key variables to determine their impact on the base case results. The analyst can ask all the "what if" questions necessary to see the affect of changes in variables such as product price, raw material costs, and operating costs on the overall results of a project. The analyst can determine which variable has the most negative or positive affect on the project's profitability. Given the possible range of a variable, such as material cost, the range of effect on the outcome can be calculated and charted. The more sensitive the outcome is to the tested variable, the more serious an error in estimating the variable would be. The purpose of sensitivity analysis is to identify the variables that have the stronger impact on the outcome of a project. Sensitivity analysis is effective in determining the consequences of a change in a variable.

Sensitivity Analysis: An Example

The following example shows sensitivity analysis by illustrating its use in breakeven analysis. Although breakeven analysis has its limitations, it is a useful analytical technique for studying the relationship among fixed costs, variable costs, and revenue. The relationship between costs and revenues must be analyzed to determine at what level of sales that total costs are covered by total revenues. Breakeven analysis indicates the point at which there is no profit or loss. The breakeven point serves as a base indication of how many units of product must be sold if a company is to avoid a loss. Figure 3-1 illustrates the breakeven concept.

In order to construct a breakeven analysis, one must have estimates of fixed costs, variable costs per unit, volume of production, and price per unit. As discussed earlier, fixed costs do not change with the level of production. Variable costs are directly related to units of production and change with the level of production. Table 3-1 shows different costs attributable to fixed costs and variable costs.

TABLE 3–1. Kinds of Costs

Fixed Costs	Variable Costs
Depreciation	Factory labor
Plant equipment	Material costs
Fixed utilities	Commissions
Rentals	Freight in and out
Debt interest	Variable factory expense
Salaries (executive and office)	Utilities (other than fixed)
Office expense	Cost of goods sold
Insurance	Sales expense

Where:

$$FC = \text{Fixed Costs}$$

$$P = \text{Sales price per unit}$$

$$Q = \text{Quantity of production in units}$$

$$V = \text{Variable cost per unit}$$

$$P-V = \text{Contribution margin}$$

$$\text{Breakeven point} = \frac{\text{Fixed Costs}}{\text{Contribution Margin}} = \frac{FC}{P-V}$$

Expressed another way:

Total Revenue = Total Cost at the breakeven point

$$TR = TC$$

Or:

$$TR - TC = 0 \text{ at the breakeven point}$$

$$TR = PQ = \text{Total Revenue}$$

$$TC = FC + VQ = \text{Total Cost}$$

Substituting:

$$PQ = FC + VQ$$

Solving for Q will derive breakeven quantity.

In a situation where a new production line is being considered, the following data might be indicated by market analysis:

$$\text{production line capacity} = 1{,}800 \text{ units}$$
$$P = \text{potential selling price} = \$200/\text{unit}$$
$$FC = \text{fixed costs} = \$50{,}000$$
$$V = \text{variable costs} = \$150/\text{unit}$$

The point at which TR = TC, the breakeven points, is 1,000 units.

$$PQ = FC + VQ$$
$$\$200(Q) = \$50{,}000 + \$150(Q)$$
$$Q = 1{,}000 \text{ units}$$

Solved another way:

$$\text{Breakeven Point by Quantity} = \frac{FC}{P - V}$$
$$= \frac{\$50{,}000}{\$200 - \$150}$$
$$= \frac{\$50{,}000}{\$50}$$
$$= 1{,}000$$

With a selling price of $200 per unit, the breakeven point is illustrated by the intersection at the lines representing total revenue and total costs (Figure 3-1).

To apply sensitivity analysis, the analyst might put in various

FIGURE 3-1. A graphic representation of the breakeven concept.

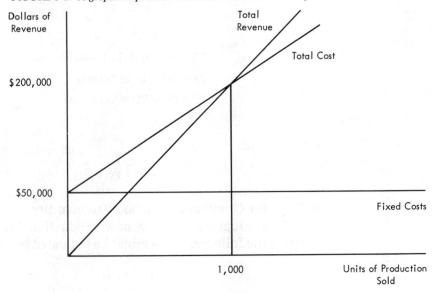

values of volume, price, variable cost, and fixed cost to measure their relative effect on profit.

$$TR \text{ (Total Revenue)} - TC \text{ (Total Cost)} = I \text{ (Profit or Loss)}$$

By substitution we find:

$$PQ - (FC + VQ) = I$$

Table 3-2 illustrates changes in volume of production of 100 unit increments above and below the breakeven point. The table also shows the impact of these changes in production on profits and that changes in the volume of production near the breakeven point result in large variations in profits and losses. Using the same basic formula shown previously, an analyst can test the sensitivity of price and profits.

$$TR - TC = I$$

$$PQ - (FC + VQ) = I$$

$$PQ - FC - VQ = I$$

TABLE 3-2. Sensitivity Analysis of Production and Profits

Volume	Profit/(Loss)*	Percent Change
500	$(25,000)	25%
600	(20,000)	33.3%
700	(15,000)	50%
800	(10,000)	100%
900	(5,000)	
1,000	0	
1,100	5,000	
1,200	10,000	100%
1,300	15,000	50%
1,400	20,000	33.3%
1,500	25,000	25%

*Losses shown in parentheses.

TABLE 3-3. Sensitivity of Analysis of Price and Profits (Volume set at 1,000 units)

Price	Profit/(Loss)*	Percent Change
$160	$(40,000)	33.3%
170	(30,000)	50%
180	(20,000)	100%
190	(10,000)	
200	0	
210	10,000	
220	20,000	100%
230	30,000	50%
240	40,000	33.3%

*Losses shown in parentheses.

Our example shows a production capacity of 1800 units with the breakeven point at 1,000 units. If market analysis shows a market potential in the range of 1,200 to 1,500 units, then the project can be considered as a very viable proposition. Further calculations can be made to estimate a range of profits based on our previous cost assumptions.

$$I(profit) = PQ - FC - VQ$$
$$Profit = \$200(1500) - \$50,000 - \$150\,(1500)$$
$$Profit = \$300,000 - \$50,000 - \$225,000$$
$$Profit = \underline{\$25,000}$$

$$Profit = \$200(1200) - \$50,000 - \$150\,(1200)$$
$$Profit = \$240,000 - \$50,000 - \$180,000$$
$$Profit = \underline{\$10,000}$$

This same information is given in Table 3-2.

The analyst can use the same calculation method and compute a minimum sales price for any level of volume. There are other variations that can be used to determine the effect of changes on profit and loss. Breakeven analysis used in this way can provide managers with a profit or loss estimate at different levels of sales and at different cost estimates. It can also approximate the effect of a change in selling prices on the company.

Sensitivity analysis can apply to other techniques of analysis as well. It may be used in capital budgeting decisions using discounted cash flows. Changes in the required rate of a return can be quickly converted into changes in the project's net present value, which represents the potential increase in wealth the project offers. The discounted cash flow method of making capital budgeting decisions will be discussed more fully in Chapter 4.

Other uses of sensitivity analysis include testing price change impact on sales plans, testing changes in the productive life of equipment, and testing the changes in demand on profitability.

RISK ANALYSIS AND COST FORECASTING

Sensitivity analysis is appropriate for asking "what if" questions and for determining the consequences of various changes in variables. Sensitivity analysis cannot, however, identify the likelihood of a change in a variable occuring. *Risk analysis* is the process used to identify and assign a degree of likelihood to changes in important variables that may be essential in determining the feasibility of a project. The economics of a project will be discussed in greater detail in Chapter 4.

The Process of Cost Forecasting

The use of cost estimates for planning purposes is very important in developing the project cost summary. The chief accounting officer of the organization should be instrumental in assembling the cost data used as a basis for a firm's activities.

As demand analysis estimates the market potential of the new project, product, or services, cost analysis determines the actual financial and technical feasibility of the proposed activity.

Cost estimates must be provided for the following categories:

1. Fixed investments such as land, buildings, fixtures, and other equipment.
2. Manufacturing costs such as direct material cost, direct labor cost, and manufacturing overhead.
3. Start-up costs such as training expenses, increased overtime, scrap expense, consulting fees, and legal fees.
4. Other related costs.

A broad series of assumptions and decisions have to be made to give a framework for developing these cost estimates. A detailed step-by-step forecasting checklist must be followed to establish accurate cost estimates. This checklist is illustrated in Table 3-4.

TABLE 3-4. Cost Forecasting Checklist

Yes	No	
_____	_____	Are the objectives of the study clearly defined?
_____	_____	Are the various alternatives clearly identified?
_____	_____	Are reliable cost estimates available for fixed investment, manufacturing costs, and other related start-up costs?
_____	_____	Are the likely changes in material costs identified?
_____	_____	Are the likely changes in labor costs identified?
_____	_____	Are the changes in unit factory overhead rates caused by the proposed production identified?
_____	_____	Has the demand analysis provided a realistic forecast of sales?
_____	_____	Have the production personnel provided estimated overhead costs for the new project based on the sales forecast?

TABLE 3-4. Cost Forecasting Checklist *(continued)*

Yes	No	
_____	_____	Have all appropriate departments submitted their budget estimates? (General and Administrative Departments, Warehousing and Distribution, Selling and Advertising, Research and Development, and so on).
_____	_____	Has a final project cost summary been completed?

Accurate cost estimates require a solid analysis of the technical requirements of the projects. Projects will vary in the depth of this type of analysis. The technological complexity of the project, the amount of resources required to accomplish the project, and the number of viable alternatives will influence the amount of attention given to the technical analysis. Most new ventures have enough "unknown" characteristics to require close attention to the specific aspects of the project in order to achieve a good cost estimates.

Technical Analysis

A large error in the technical study of a project can have significant impact. An inadequate technical study can lead to an immediate failure of the new venture or to costly readjustment of project goals. The estimates of manufacturing costs, investment requirements, start-up costs, and other related expenses need an accurate technical study.

The technical study should include the following seven steps:

Step One
Yes   No

_____ _____   Will the process work? Can the product be produced? Can the service be delivered?

In some cases experiments, research, or tests are required to determine if a new product or process is workable.

Step Two
Yes   No

_____ _____   Are proper inventory estimates made?

Proper inventory levels are necessary to meet demand requirements and to maintain an even production schedule. The necessary inventory level must be known in order to make the appropriate cost estimates for inventory requirements.

Manufacturing firms usually have three types of inventory:

1. Raw Materials.   Raw materials and component parts are influenced by production schedules, anticipated sales, reliability of supply sources, quantity discounts, and price volitility.

2. Work in process.   This type of inventory consists of the partially complete products located in the plant. The level of work in process inventory is affected by the characteristics of the production process particularly its length. This type of inventory is necessary for a smooth production schedule.

3. Finished goods.   The level of finished products in stock depends on the right balance between production and sales. A safety stock is necessary to insure that there is no delay in filling customer orders. Also, finished goods will build up when sales fluctuate and levels of production do not. Inventories of this type are used for production stabilization purposes.

Inventory levels should be estimated to minimize the total cost of ordering inventory and holding inventory. Estimating inventories at approximately 10% of the forecasted annual demand provided by the market analysis is a good rule of thumb.

Step Three
Yes   No

_____ _____   Has the production schedule been developed?

The projected production requirements are required to establish a production schedule. The market analysis should provide estimates of monthly or quarterly sales that can be used for this purpose. After a production schedule has been developed, tangible production cost estimates can be made and prepared for the project cost summary. The cost of the production process must include the total sequence of operations and functions required to convert raw material inventory into finished good inventory. This should include the cost of:

- production equipment
- handling equipment (conveyors, hoists, cranes, and so on.)
- space requirements
- inventory levels
- personnel (production and supervision)
- delivery
- inspection
- maintenance

Step three leads necessarily to steps four, five, and six.

Step Four

Yes   No

_____   _____   Are special tools and equipment necessary?

If the answer is "yes," steps must be taken to analyze the costs related to these necessary items. Cost information concerning special tools and equipment can be obtained from:

- equipment manufacturers
- trade literature
- other manufacturers using the same or similar equipment
- trade associations

In some cases a capital budgeting analysis of equipment alternatives is necessary. Since present cost cannot be compared dollar for dollar with future costs, an equivalent annual cost in present value terms should be used to choose among alternatives. The present value method of discounting future cost amounts will be discussed and illustrated in Chapter 4.

Step Five

Yes   No

_____   _____   Have labor requirements and costs been established?

Accurate cost estimates require the knowledge of how many employees are required and the rates at which the various skill levels must be paid. This information can be used to determine final labor costs. Total workload requirements are estimated for each skill level classification. These totals are then multiplied by the appropriate pay rate for that skill level. In addition to direct production labor, factory overhead must be included. Typical types of factory overhead include

- maintenance
- inspection
- supervision
- receiving
- packing
- shipping
- control
- analysis
- safety
- quality control

Step Six
Yes   No

_____ _____   Have the various space requirements and costs been estalished?

Most projects will require various types of space considerations. Most common are:

- production space
- sales space
- administrative space
- other service space

Production space includes work areas, storage areas, and testing areas. Layout charts and process charts can be helpful in calculating the actual square footage of space required.

Other space requirements should be reasonably estimated to calculate building or rental costs. These other areas include:

- administrative offices
- meeting rooms
- sales areas
- training rooms
- accounting and auditing areas
- safety office
- security office
- break rooms (showers, lunch area, and so on)
- research and development area
- purchasing area
- quality control
- engineering
- maintenance
- warehouse space
- toolroom
- personnel offices

If the project requires the decision to build a building, then that aspect of the project should be approached as a feasibility project within a project. The same basic steps should be followed to examine the market factors, the cost factors, and the financial considerations of a new site location.

Step Seven
Yes   No

_____ _____   Has the project cost summary been completed?

The cost estimates obtained through the other steps in this process are important in determining the financial feasibility of the decision. The integrity of the financial analysis and the estimated return on investments depends on the accuracy of the market analysis (sales estimates) and the cost analysis (cost estimates).

TABLE 3-5. Project Cost Summary

Category	Quantity	Description	Monthly	Annual
Fixed investments		Land	___	___
		Construction cost	___	___
		Building cost	___	___
		Security systems	___	___
		Fire prevention systems	___	___
		Furniture	___	___
		Fixtures	___	___
		Production equipment	___	___
		Office equipment	___	___
		Trucks	___	___
Manufacturing costs		Direct material	___	___
		Direct labor	___	___
		Factory overhead	___	___
		Maintenance	___	___
		Utilities	___	___
		Quality control	___	___
		Office supplies	___	___
		Rent	___	___
		Insurance	___	___
		Telephone	___	___
		Depreciation	___	___
		Taxes	___	___
		Supervision	___	___
		Toolroom	___	___
		Miscellaneous expenses	___	___
Start-up Costs		Financing expense	___	___
		Consultants' fees	___	___
		Training	___	___
		Waste	___	___
		Delay expense	___	___
		Travel	___	___
		Legal fees	___	___
		Patents	___	___
Other related Costs		Working capital requirements	___	___
		Extraordinary expenses	___	___
		Administrative expense	___	___
		Salaries	___	___
		Insurance	___	___
		Supplies	___	___
	TOTAL COST		═══	═══

These analyses should provide the parameters to determine return on investment (ROI).

The project cost summary must include the basic cost elements mentioned at the beginning of the forecasting portion of this chapter. They are:

1. Fixed investments
2. Manufacturing costs
3. Start-up costs
4. Other related costs

Table 3-5 illustrates an example of a project cost summary including the four basic cost elements.

The project cost summary provides the information necessary for a projected statement of the cost of goods sold. This coupled with information from the market analysis provides the basis for the pro forma income statement. This estimates the profitability of the project. Pro forma income statements are exhibited in Appendix B. Additional aids can now be produced to help the planner such as pro forma balance sheets, cash flow projections, and detailed cost summaries.

PROCEDURES

Forecasting Procedures

Cost forecasting can utilize many of the tools described in Chapter 2 in relation to forecasting sales. Developing cost forecasts of totally new ventures for which there is no historical cost figures is more difficult and subject to greater error than forecasts for projects that have cost histories.

The correct procedure to forecast costs varies from project to project. The objective of cost forecasting is to approximate the real expenses involved in an undertaking so that profitability can be projected. The actual procedure for forecasting cost may be determined by an examination of the objectives and resources of the principles to the venture.

Several forecasting techniques can be used to estimate costs. A discussion follows.

Judgement techniques. The various experiences of key personnel have led to "rules of thumb" that can determine certain kinds of costs in some cases. These techniques are subjective in nature and should not be the sole basis for cost analysis.

Survey techniques. Just as market information can be acquired through consumer surveys, so can cost information. Personal or telephone interviews with persons with experience in the appropriate field are normally used. Such a survey of expert opinion can generate helpful cost data.

Historical data techniques. When historical data is available, cost forecasting can be accomplished by making certain subjective assumptions and then projecting historical cost elements into the future.

Historical data is used for *trend analysis*. Trend analysis makes use of hand calculators which are programmed or programmable to project past points of costs to specific future dates. A simple technique of plotting the past cost history of a certain cost element can be helpful. The scatter diagram technique (Fig. 3-2) charts cost data for a number of periods. A line is drawn midway between high and low points. This line is called the *line of best fit* or the *regression line*. Be certain to keep in mind that many costs are distinct entities and cannot be projected in the same way sales can.

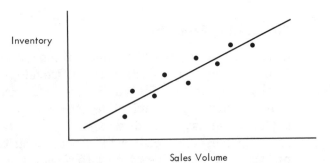

FIGURE 3-2. Scatter Diagram

A more sophisticated approach to forecasting is *multiple regression*. In simple regression, a cost is assumed to be the function of only one variable. In multiple regression the cost or dependent variable is dependent on a number of variables. Multiple regression was illustrated in Chapter 2.

Percent of Sales. Many costs can be adequately expressed in the form of a percent of sales. One such expense that can be calculated as a percentage of sales is sales commissions. A good sales forecast is essential for this method of estimating costs. The percent of sales method implies a linear relationship between sales and the expense item being calculated. Not only can certain expense items be forecast as a percentage of sales, but also balance sheet items and external financing requirements can be developed by this method.

SUMMARY

Accurately estimating cost is extremely important to establish the feasibility of any project. Cost overruns are common and often disasterous to the principles involved in a venture. Every attempt should be made to *identify* and *estimate* accurately all costs involved in a project to avoid failure. This is accomplished best by a thorough technical study and an accompanying cost forecast. The results of forecasting process should yield a project cost summary which can be used in determining return on investment, the subject of Chapter 4.

RETURN ON
INVESTMENT

The final and perhaps overriding consideration in determining the feasibility of a project is the potential profitability it represents. The previous chapters have dealt with the analysis of market potential and the forecasting of costs. In this chapter we will focus on the financial and risk analytical techniques which can be used to insure profitable investment decisions.

One of the major objectives of all the time, energy, and resources marshalled toward a project is to generate a "good" profit. Just what is considered to be a "good" profit is sometimes a matter of personal judgement. However, it is advisable to establish certain levels of return on investment that will be acceptable for choosing among project alternatives.

WHAT IS RETURN ON INVESTMENT?

Simply stated, return on investment (ROI) is how much the investment returns to you on an annual basis. It is the most meaningful and popular measure of economic success. The term ROI is widely understood by accountants, financial analysts, bankers, managers, and investors. ROI analysis is very helpful in determining the health of a project. ROI itself does not measure the safety of an investment, only its performance expressed as a percentage.

Return on investment can be calculated by dividing net profit by the total investment required to generate the profit. The following formula illustrates the calculation of ROI:

$$\text{Return on Investment (ROI)} = \frac{\text{Net Profit}}{\text{Total Investment}}$$

$$\text{ROI} = 20.5\% = \frac{\$37,500}{\$182,350}$$

ROI can be calculated for a wide range of investments including saving accounts, profit centers, division, and entire companies.

A second approach to return on investment is known as the *duPont system of financial analysis*. This method brings together the profitability margin on sales and the activity ratio of asset (investment) turnover. This approach to ROI takes into consideration the combination of the efficient use of assets (investments) and the profit margin on sales. It has been widely accepted in American industry.

Return on investment can also be expressed as a combination

of the profit margin on sales and the turnover activity ratio of an investment:

Net profits divided by sales equals the profit margin.

$$\frac{\text{Net Profit}}{\text{Sales}} = \text{Profit Margin}$$

Sales divided by investment = Turnover of assets

$$\frac{\text{Sales}}{\text{Investment}} = \text{Turnover}$$

Return on investment is equal to Turnover × Profit Margin

$$\frac{\text{Net Profit}}{\text{Sales}} \times \frac{\text{Sales}}{\text{Investment}} = \text{ROI}$$

FINANCIAL ANALYSIS PROCESS

Financial analysis and capital budgeting consist of the process of selecting among alternative investments in land, buildings, productive equipment, or other assets for future gain. Since decisions of this type usually commit the firm to a long term course of action, careful analysis is required to identify the potential return.

Theoretically, capital budgeting is very simple. You just list all the investment opportunities available, rank them according to profitability, and accept all investments up to the point at which marginal benefits equal marginal cost. However, in reality the complexity of revolving planning timetables makes the choice of capital outlays more difficult. Varying project length, start-up time, and payout create difficulty in comparing investment opportunity.

The depth of the economic analysis depends on the type of project, its urgency, and the objectives of the firm. For example, a burned out generator in a power plant must be replaced. The decision is not replacement vs. nonreplacement. The decision would be what particular generator is most productive, least costly, or most readily available.

Before we discuss in detail the analytical techniques for determining profitability and for making capital decisions, a framework for the decision process should be established. We list the steps of a *Decision Flow Chart* and follow with an explanation of each step.

- Step one: Define problem.
- Step two: Identify alternative.
- Step three: Identify relevant costs and revenues that will change because of the action taken.
- Step four: Determine the alternative that has the most beneficial result.

Step one: Problem Definition. This first step is self-explanatory. However, even though it is so elementary, it is often overlooked. Many times a statement of a problem such as "The problem is we need more trucks" is not a problem statement at all. It is a suggested alternative solution. Too often decision makers jump prematurely to step two without clearly articulating the problem. The importance of proper problem definition cannot be over-emphasized. Replacement of a worn-out piece of equipment, development of a new product, and construction of a new plant each creates a uniquely complex problem to overcome. Each example generally produces several alternatives. These alternatives must be clearly identified and evaluated.

Step two: Identification of Alternatives. Alternative actions can range all the way from doing nothing, going out of business, replacing with the same type of equipment, replacing with different equipment, replacing with larger or smaller equipment, and so on. From the wide range of available alternatives, only the appropriate alternatives should be selected for further analysis.

Step three: Identification of Relevant Costs and Revenues. We must identify the relevant costs and revenues that will change as a result of the action taken. Chapter three dealt with many of the aspects of technical analysis and cost forecasting that also apply to this step in the capital budgeting process. It is inappropriate to assume that past operating costs will apply to new ventures. Although it is tempting to simply project historical cost into the future, it is very hazardous to do so. Methods of dealing with the uncertainty surrounding the cost and revenue flows involved in capital budgeting must be incorporated to realistically identify and estimate costs of revenues. These methods are discussed in this chapter.

The basic question asked in step three is, "What are the changes in costs and revenues that will occur because of an action taken?" Other questions to be answered are

What additional revenues will be generated?
What revenues will be lost?

What is the *net* impact of the action on revenue?
What additional costs will be generated?
What costs will be eliminated?
What is the *net* impact of the action on costs?

The preceding questions lead us to the economic principle of incremental changes in cash flow. The focus is on the economic cash flow concept. Once an after-tax cash flow change is determined we are ready for step four.

Step four: Determination of Most Beneficial Alternative. The capital budgeting decision alternative with the greatest positive return on investment is generally considered to be superior. The specific method of analysis used to calculate the alternative having the optimum economic return over the life of the investment must in some way take into account the trade-off of current cash outlay and future cash inflow.

THE METHODS OF ANALYZING INVESTMENTS

There are many methods available for evaluating investment alternatives. Much has been written and many models prepared concerning the capital budgeting decision. A discussion of some of the more common methods follows.

The focus of capital budgeting is to make decisions that maximize the value of a firm's investment. We must choose a method that will answer most appropriately the question, "Which is the most profitable alternative?" The most common criteria for choosing among alternatives are *non-time value methods* and *time value methods*. Each of these methods has its advantages and disadvantages which will be discussed along with the description of each method.

Three concepts commonly associated with non-time value methods are

- Payback period
- Simple return on investment
- Average return on investment

Three concepts commonly associated with time value methods are

- Net present value
- Internal rate of return
- Present value index

The Payback Period

The payback period is simply an estimate of how long it will take for the investment to pay for itself. No interest factors are included in the calculations. Once the payback period is determined, it is usually compared with a rule of thumb or a standard period. If it is determined that the investment will pay for itself in less time than the standard period the investment would be made. In deciding between mutually exclusive alternatives, the one with the shortest payback period is generally chosen.

The payback period can be calculated in several ways. The most common one is with the formula:

$$\text{Payback} = \frac{\text{Net investment outlay}}{\text{Net annual cash flow benefits}}$$

When annual cash flow benefits are irregular or investment outlay comes in various time frames, information such as shown in Table 4-1 shows the payback period as four years.

TABLE 4-1.

Year	Investment outlay	Annual cash flow benefits	Cumulative cash flow
1	$120,000	$22,000	$−(98,000)
2	0	47,000	−(51,000)
3	11,500	34,500	−(28,000)
4	0	28,000	0
5	0	29,000	+29,000
6	0	23,000	+52,000
7	0	14,000	+66,000

The payback period method of calculation is easy to calculate and as a result has been widely used. With this method, projects

The payback period method of calculation is easy to calculate and as a result has been widely used. With this method, projects with shortest payback period are usually chosen. However, because it does not take into consideration the time value of money, the payback period method has serious flaws of logic.

ADVANTAGES
1. Ease of calculation.
2. More favorable short-run effects on earnings per share because of short payback period.
3. The method is easily understood.

DISADVANTAGES
1. The method completely ignores all cash flows beyond the payback period.
2. It does not adjust for risk related to uncertainty.
3. It ignores the time value of money.

Some firms are beginning to use the payback method in combination with one or more of the time value methods described below. When this is done, the payback period is used as a risk measurement while the time value method is used as an indicator of profitability.

Simple Return on Investment

The simple return on investment is an outgrowth of the logic of the payback method. The method can be represented by manipulating the payback formula. It is an attempt to express the desirability of an investment in terms of a percentage return on the original investment outlay.

$$\text{Return on investment} = \frac{\text{Net annual cash flow benefits}}{\text{Net investment outlay}}$$

The simple ROI method has all the drawbacks and disadvantages of the payback method. No reference at all is made to the economic life of the project. An investment of $50,000 with an average annual benefit of $5,000 will yield a 10% return regardless of whether the length of the project is one, five, or ten years.

$$\text{ROI} = \frac{\$5,000}{\$50,000} = 10\%$$

Average Return on Investment

The expected average rate of return is a measure of the estimated profitability of an investment. This calculation differs from the simple return of investment by employing the average net investment.

$$\text{Average return on investment} = \frac{\text{Net annual cash flow benefits}}{\text{Average net investment outlay}}$$

With assuming straight-line depreciation and no residual value at the end of its life, an average investment would be equal to one-half of the original investment. This takes into consideration the effect of depreciation on the amount of the investment. Using the example above, a net annual cash flow of $5,000 on an original expenditure of $50,000 would be 20%, not 10%.

$$\text{Average ROI} = \frac{\$\ 5,000}{25,000} = 20\%$$

Advanced Concept of Analysis:
Time Value Methods

The investment decision values involves the trade-off between current dollar outlays and future benefits over a period of time. As a result, it is not prudent to ignore the timing of the benefits of investment alternatives. In this regard, the quicker the return the better. It is obviously preferable to receive benefits quickly and defer the expenditure outlays. Money has value directly related to the timing of its receipt or disbursement. The delay of receiving money means an opportunity cost in terms of lost income.

The Net Present Value Method

The basic idea of the *net present value* (NPV) method is to overcome the disadvantages of non-time value methods. The NPV method provides a balance of the trade-off between investment outlays and future benefits in terms of time adjusted dollars. The present value of discounted cash flows is an amount at present which is equivalent to a project's cash flow for a particular interest rate. Generally, the interest rate used to discount future cash flows is a company's cost of capital rate. The net present value method involves

1. determining the present value of the net investment cost outlay.
2. estimating the future cash flow benefits.
3. discounting the future cash flows to present value at the appropriate cost of capital.
4. subtracting the present value of the costs from the present value of the benefits.

If the amount derived from Step 4 is positive, then the investment is considered to be a profitable investment, since the time-adjusted internal rate of return of the investment is greater than the cost of capital. Conversely, a negative figure indicates that the project is earning a rate of return less than the cost of capital chosen by the firm as a standard of decision.

55

The net present value can be calculated by the following formula:

$$NPV = \frac{R_1}{(1 + i)^1} + \frac{r_2}{(1 + i)^2} + \cdots + \frac{R_n}{(1 + i)^n} - IC$$

Where:

NPV = The net present value of the investment

R = The expected dollar returns or cash flows each year

i = The appropriate interest rate (cost of capital)

IC = The present value (PV) of the investment cost

n = The project's expected life

The net present values of two alternative projects are shown in Table 4-2.

TABLE 4–2. Net Present Values of Alternative Projects

Year	Net return or cash flow		Interest factor $(1 + i)^n$	Present value of cash flow	
			PROJECT 1		
1	$300	×	0.91	$ 273	
2	400	×	0.3	332	
3	500	×	0.75	375	
4	700	×	0.68	476	
				$1,456	PV of inflows
				1,200	− PV of cost
				$ 256	Net Present Value
			PROJECT 2		
1	$700	×	0.91	$ 637	
2	200	×	0.83	166	
3	300	×	0.75	225	
4	400	×	0.68	272	
				$1,300	PV of inflows
				1,200	− PV of cost
				$ 100	Net Present Value

The project that has the highest return is Project 1, even though the payback period of Project 2 is identical. The greatest benefit will be provided by selecting Project 1. If the two projects are not mutually exclusive and funds are available, both investment opportunities should be accepted.

The present value method has several advantages which make it more suitable than the payback methods as a basis of comparing investments.

ADVANTAGES

1. It considers the time value of money.
2. It concentrates the values of costs and benefits in a comparable time frame.
3. It is fairly simple to understand and calculate.

DISADVANTAGES

1. It assumes benefits and costs can be estimated for the lifetime of the project.
2. It requires equal time periods for comparison of several investment alternatives.
3. It is sensitive to changes in the interest rate used to discount the values.

Internal Rate of Return (IRR)

The *internal rate of return* is simply the yield of a project. The IRR is defined as the interest rate that discounts the future cash flows, or receipts, and makes them equal to the initial cost outlay. The time value of money is taken into consideration. The same formula that was used for net present value can be used with one slight variation. Instead of solving for net present value, the present value of the cost is made equal to the present value of the benefits. The equation is solved for the interest rate that will make the present value of the cost equal to the present value of the benefits. Stated another way, the internal rate of return of a project is the discount interest rate that generates a net present value of zero. Below is the NPV formula and the change necessary to create the IRR formula.

NPV Formula

$$NPV = \frac{R_1}{(1+i)^1} + \frac{R_2}{(1+i)^2} + \ldots + \frac{R_n}{(1+i)^n} - IC$$

IRR Formula

$$\frac{R_1}{(1+i)^1} + \frac{R_2}{(1+i)^2} + \ldots + \frac{R_n}{(1+i)^n} = IC$$

$$0 = \frac{R_1}{(1+i)^1} + \frac{R_2}{(1+i)^2} + \cdots + \frac{R_n}{(1+i)^n} - IC$$

Solve for i, then $i = IRR$

In the new formula for IRR, i represents the interest rate that equates the present values of the benefits and the costs of a project. In the NPV formula, i represents the firm's cost of capital. When the cost of capital is used in the formula and NPV = O, then the internal rate of return is equal to the cost of capital. When NPV is positive, the IRR is greater than the cost of capital. When NPV is negative, the IRR is less than the cost of capital. Whenever the IRR is greater than the firm's cost of capital, the investment is a positive one. The IRR can be found by trial and error. The IRR method is widely accepted as a ranking device. The yield is reasonably accurate and much superior to the simple payback and simple return on investment methods.

ADVANTAGES
1. Because the IRR method is closely related to the NPV method, it is familiar to many business practioners. This makes the method more readily accepted.
2. Calculation of the firm's cost of capital is *not* required as it is with the NPV method.
3. The method time-values money.

DISADVANTAGES
1. The internal rate of return does not do a good job of comparing investments having large differences in magnitude. For example, a $20,000 investment with an IRR of 42 percent cannot be compared with an investment of $100,000 with an IRR of 30 percent. It may be far better to marshall all resources toward the $100,000 investment even though the IRR is lower than the other investment.
2. In the same manner, length of the life of the investment is also important. It may be more advantageous to invest funds at a lower IRR for a longer term than to invest short term for a slightly higher IRR. The pertinent criticism of the IRR method is that it assumed that reinvestment can be made at the IRR, which may not be possible.

Present Value Index

This method is similar to the present value method. A ratio is determined between the present value of the cash flow benefits and the present values of the net investment outlays. The *present value index* is sometimes referred to as the benefit/cost ratio of discounted cash flows. Several alternative projects may have similar NPV's but require widely different investment amounts. To choose an alternative simply on the size of NPV would ignore the relative different sizes of the projects. Equal NPV's coming from different size investments will have different IRR's.

A formal way of expressing this difference is to compare the projects on a benefits/costs basis.

$$\text{Present Value Index} = \frac{\text{Present Value of Cash Flow Benefits}}{\text{Present Value of Net Investment Outlay}}$$

The higher the index, the better the project. However, any PV index over 1.0 beats the minimum standard built into the calculation of PV and should be funded. However, most projects are competing for limited funds. Table 4-3 gives examples of the present value index.

TABLE 4-3. **Present Value Index**

Alternative	Present Value of Benefits	Present Value of Costs	Net Present Value	PV Index
1	$10,400	$ 8,800	$ 1,600	1.18
2	15,000	13,000	2,000	1.15
3	15,000	13,400	1,600	1.12
4	17,500	18,800	−(1,300)	.93
5	15,000	12,000	3,000	1.25

Table 4-3 illustrates a comparison of the PV Index and the NPV ranking methods. Slightly different results are given. Notice that Alternatives 1 and 3 have the same NPV, but Alternative 1 has the higher PV index and is, therefore, more favorable. The advantages and disadvantages of the PV index method are similar to those listed for the net present value method.

RISK ANALYSIS

The classical definition of the riskiness of an asset is the probability that the expected future returns will fall below predicted levels. This is often measured by the standard deviation (or the coefficient of variation) of expected returns. Earlier we discussed only the informal treatment of risk resulting from making judgement estimates of economic life and cash flow amounts in our discussion of the methods of making capital budget decisions. Some situations call for a more formal treatment of assessing risk and the effects of uncertainty. We referred to sensitivity analysis in Chapter 3. Sensitivity analysis can be used to calculate a project's NPV's under alternative assumptions to determine how sensitive NPV is to changing circumstances.

Projects having large variability in expected returns require an even more formal approach to dealing with risk. Risk analysis attempts to identify the likelihood of events occurring. Risk results from lack of experience, misinterpretation of data, bias in forecasting, errors in analysis, and changes in economic conditions. In project feasibility analysis there are usually a number of variables that must be considered.

More than seven out of ten surveyed companies report that they employ some type of risk analysis in project analysis. Some of the most common risk analysis techniques are risk adjusted discount rate or rate or return, risk adjusted cash flows, risk adjusted payback periods.

Risk Adjusted Discount Rate

One of the most frequently used methods is the risk adjusted discount rate method. The basic objective of the risk adjusted discount rate method is to increase the applied discount rate when dealing with risky projects. If the simple rate of return method is being used, the cut-off rate is raised to allow for a greater "cushion" for risky projects. The increase in the discount rate, also known as cost of capital, is a risk premium to protect the firm from uncertainty of future cash flows of uncertain investments.

As mentioned earlier, the variability of the probability distributions of expected returns can be estimated. In some cases, the probability distribution can be estimated objectively with statistical techniques. However, there are many situations when the estimates must be determined subjectively by subjective probability distributions. Once the probability distributions are determined, the variability of the distribution can be measured by standard deviation or coefficient of variation. The project with the larger deviation represents the greatest risk and is assigned the higher discount rate.

The effect of the higher discount rate is to reduce the present value of the future benefits and to make it more difficult for a risky investment to achieve a positive net present value. Marginal projects that are risky are consequently rejected. The risk adjusted discount rate method is easy to apply, but it has some disadvantages. Usually the adjusted rate applies to all costs and revenues, even those that can be estimated with relative certainty. The lack of discrimination among the cost and revenue estimates is the major criticism of this method.

Risk Adjusted Cash Flows

As forecasts are being made to develop the point estimate or most likely estimate, the analyst will incorporate into the estimate the risk he perceives. He then defines the degree of uncertainty in terms of probability of occurrence. For example, an optimistic, most likely, and pessimistic estimate are made taking historical data, environmental analysis, and expected trends into consideration. This three-level method of forecasting was developed in Chapter 2. To illustrate, consider the following calculation of the expected value of the cash flows from two projects in Table 4-4.

TABLE 4-4. Project Cash Flows and Probabilities

Alternative	Cash Flow	Probability of Economic Condition
Project 1	$750	.2 Recession
	600	.5 Normal
	300	.3 Boom
		1.0
Project 2	$250	.2 Recession
	800	.5 Normal
	400	.3 Boom
		1.0

Table 4-5 shows the calculation of expected value based on the data of Table 4-4.

TABLE 4-5. Expected Value of Cash Flow

Alternative	Cash Flow	Probability of Economic Condition	Expected Value
Project 1	$750	.2 Recession	$150
	600	.5 Normal	300
	300	.3 Boom	90
		1.0	$540
Project 2	$250	.2 Recession	$ 50
	800	.5 Normal	400
	400	.3 Boom	120
		1.0	$570

The expected value of the cash flows of Project 1 is $540 instead of the $600 point estimate, while the expected value of the cash flows of Project 2 is $570 rather than $800. The expected value gives the forecaster and decision maker a better feeling for the risk involved in the decision.

The risk adjusted cash flow is generally lower than the best estimate cash flow. The effect of using a risk adjusted cash flow in the net present value method of capital budgeting is a lower net present value than that which would have been obtained by using the best estimate cash flow. The result is that marginal projects with risky potential benefit are more readily discarded.

SIMULATION MODELS

Computer simulation can be used to extend probability concepts in decision making. The computer allows for decision makers to estimate, for each of a dozen or so variables of major products, ranges of possible outcomes and the probability distributions for these ranges. Focus might be placed on sales volume, prices, key cost elements, salvage values, interest rate fluctuations, or cash flows. A series of outcomes of the project is then developed by the computer simulation. The computer output will allow statements to be made such as, "There is a 65 percent likelihood that the net present value of the project will be $200,000" or "There is a one in ten chance that the project will lose $210,000." The sophistication of this analysis and the unlimited number of variables place obvious limitations on its use. These include:

1. The natural tendency to oversimplify the variables.
2. The selection of a large number of assumptions.
3. The use of specialized and expensive equipment and personnel to develop programs and carry out the technique.
4. The fact that simulation is time consuming and leads to time lags.

COST ANALYSIS FOR NOT-FOR-PROFIT ENTITIES

The concept of "not-for-profit entites" is very broad. It includes many different types of economic organizations such as churches, government organizations, universities, hospitals, charitable institutions, clubs, fraternal groups, and cooperatives. Income, which is the traditional measure of success for a profit entity, is a poor measure of efficiency for an organization that does not intend to make profits. Traditional breakeven analysis is a difficult concept to apply to not-for-profit entities (see Chapter 3).

Projects of any economic organization should be evaluated for their ability to meet the objectives of the organization within the budget constraints and incomes generated by the activity.

With not-for-profit entities this is complicated by the inability to express their services in dollar terms.

Benefit/Cost Analysis

Cost analysis for not-for-profit organizations is difficult because some costs are difficult to assign. When a nonprofit organization is choosing between alternative programs that fall within the scope of their objectives, benefit/cost (B/C) analysis can be helpful. Benefit/cost analysis is a formalized attempt to obtain the maximum benefits from a given level of funding. At a given level of supportable funding, a community will want the best possible police protection; a university will want the best faculty; the Red Cross will want the most effective blood donor recruiting program. Benefit/cost analysis allows a nonprofit organization to evaluate various alternatives.

Each program can be evaluated based on a comparison of benefit/cost ratios. For example, a public library may be considered the addition of a new business section, a film rental library, or an arts library. These alternatives are exhibited in Table 4-6.

TABLE 4-6. Benefit/Cost Analysis

Alternative	Benefits	Costs	Net Benefit	B/C Ratio
1	$27,500	$25,000	$2,500	1.1
2	42,000	37,000	5,000	1.3
3	12,500	16,500	(4,000)	.76

Alternatives 1 and 2 have a positive net benefit, and a benefit/cost ratio greater than one. Alternative 2 has the most favorable benefit/cost ratio. However, if the library has approximately $70,000 available, it should embark on both alternatives. Alternative 3 fails both the net benefit test and the B/C ratio test. Unless there are other overriding considerations, alternative three should be rejected.

The basic disadvantage of this type of analysis is the difficulty of estimating both costs and benefits. Costs are perhaps the easiest part of the equation. Cost of construction, equipment, supplies, salaries, and the like can usually be accurately estimated. Social costs are more difficult to appraise. On the other hand, benefit analysis poses many difficult problems. As we attempt to identify each type of benefit, we run into some social, aesthetic, and nonmonetary benefits. How these are assigned dollar values radically influences the B/C analysis.

Cost-Effectiveness Analysis

When there is difficulty comparing alternatives on the benefit/cost basis, cost effectiveness analysis may be appropriate. Cost effectiveness analysis deals with the effect of variations in cost on benefit. The focus of this analysis is to determine how effective an operation is rather than trying to see how much more benefit there is than cost.

SUMMARY

This chapter has dealt with the process and methods of making capital budgeting decisions. The final consideration of the feasibility decision is, "How profitable will the project be?" The concepts of return on investment are essential to answering this question. The final question is, "Is the project feasible?" Hopefully the analysis has led to a clear "yes" or a clear "no." In some cases, an "I don't know" will be the response. To answer the question "yes" implies that the market exists; costs are identifiable and controllable; the process or service works; the financial returns on the investment are satisfactory; the uncertainty is tolerable; and funds are available. The "yes" response, then, requires mobilization, action, and the sequencing of strategic activities to proceed with the project.

PREPARING
THE
FINAL REPORT

Once the feasibility study has been completed, a written report of the study is usually prepared. If the project proves feasible and outside funding is needed, it is especially important to prepare a good written report.

WRITTEN REPORTS

The Small Business Administration, many commercial investors, and individual investors require that a feasibility report be presented with any request for funds. Even if the feasibility study is done "in-house," a written report should be prepared for future reference and for evaluation of different techniques used in carrying out the study.

Most written reports contain the following parts or sections:

Certification—if prepared by an outside party
Executive Summary
Scope and Limitations
Assumptions
Body of the Report
Technical Appendices

Certification

The certification statement is needed only when a feasibility study is done by people outside the organization. It is a statement which certifies that the party (1) does not have any personal interests (monetary interests) in the project and that (2) all the information in the report is accurate. A typical statement would read as follows:

We, the undersigned, do hereby certify that we have no personal monetary interests in the proposed project. We further certify that all the information contained in this report is accurate subject to the limitations and assumptions set forth in the report.

_____
Robert E. Stevens

_____
Philip K. Sherwood

One reason for such a statement is to identify the role of the preparer of the report as one who can deal with the people purchasing the report in an objective or "arm's length" manner. Another reason for a statement of certification is to testify to the accuracy of the data which is contained in the report. Such statements would be especially important if third party financing was to be sought.

Executive Summary

The executive summary or abstract of the report summarizes the entire report in one or two pages. This not only prepares the reader of the report for the main body of the study but this is what many people who will be exposed to the report are interested in— "How does the study turn out in the end?"

The executive summary can be organized around four basic questions which, in essence, constitute the information readers are interested in:

Is there sufficient demand to warrant this proposed project?

Can demand be supplied at reasonable cost in terms of production resources and techniques?

Can the project be operated at a profit?

Will the level of profits generated by the project be sufficient to justify the investment?

A paragraph or two on each of these questions summarizes the report in a logical fashion which follows the way the body of the report is written. These are salient questions in the minds of the readers of the report.

Scope and Limitations

The scope and limitations section of the report spells out what areas are to be covered in the feasibility study and the limitations relating to the data collected or to appropriate applications of the findings. For example, if the management of the proposed project has not been identified, a statement is usually made that it is beyond the scope of the study to analyze the project's management. This is a statement of warning to the reader that no analysis of managerial skills has been undertaken.

If primary data was collected by telephone, a limiting statement may be made about how the sample fails to include people without phones or with an unlisted number. If the purchase of a large track of land were proposed and no recent land sales of that nature had recently occurred, then a limiting statement may be made about how land costs were calculated.

In essence, the scope and limitations help the reader understand the circumstances under which conclusions were drawn and that other circumstances may have resulted in different conclusions. the reader is cautioned about inappropriate application of this particular study to other, different circumstances.

Assumptions

A study is only as good as the assumptions upon which it is based. It is imperative that assumptions be made about various events that impact highly on the feasibility of the project during the course of the planning period. Assumptions must be made about those events which are beyond the control of the analyst but whose change, occurance, or failure of occurance alter the effectiveness or efficiency of the project.

While the types of appropriate assumptions vary greatly from project to project, some examples of the types of assumptions needed are as follows: No new competitors will enter the market within the next year. No price controls will be used in this market within the next year. The shortages experienced during the last year in raw materials will continue until the need of the planning period. An experienced manager will be hired to manage the new operation. Each of the assumptions deals with events which are beyond the control of the analyst but which when altered would greatly impact on the feasibility of a given project.

The Body of the Report

The body of the report presents the detailed discussion of the findings of the feasibility study. One common method of oganization follows the steps used to complete a feasibility study and a chapter by chapter coverage of the various topics. The chapters might be titled as follows:

Chapter 1:	Demand Analysis
Chapter 2:	Supply Analysis
Chapter 3:	Return on Investment Analysis or Breakeven Analysis
Chapter 4:	Summary and Conclusions

If the management of the proposed project has been identified, then an additional chapter may be added after the analysis of return on investment. This chapter would present the background of each of the members of the management team including education, training, experience, and stock ownership, if any. This is done to support the "management feasibility" of the project. In other words, this chapter would attempt to analyze the level of management skills which would be used to run the project, if indeed, the project were feasible.

Appendices

Because many readers may not be interested in the details of how demand was forecast, most reports will provide for technical or supporting materials in appendices. For example, some readers may have the skill to analyze whether proper techniques were used, but such material is not included in the body of the report so as not to delay the majority of readers.

The appendices may contain documents supporting the need for the projects, bids from equipment suppliers, land appraisals, building estimates, or other material which contain supportive detail for statements made in the body of the report.

SELECTING A WRITING STYLE

One decision that must be made before preparing the report is which writing style is appropriate. There are two basic styles used in preparing feasibility studies: the popular style and the technical style. The basic factor that determines the chosen style is the audience who will read the report. As a general rule, reports using the popular style are prepared for people outside the organization such as bankers and potential investors or for people outside a department such as an investment committee or top management. Internal reports prepared to be read only by others with similar technical backgrounds commonly use the technical style.

The popular report is written in "layman's" language and it is assumed that the reader does not have a background necessary to handle the technical material which may be a part of the analysis. Technical material is put into appendices at the end of the report as supporting documents of material included in the body of the report. If, for example, demand is analyzed using multiple regression analysis, the method used to identify the independent variables and to derive the specific regression coefficients may be described in an appendix. Only the results of the analysis are presented in the body of the report.

If the technical style is used, the writer assumes that the reader has sufficient technical knowledge, so the technical material is included in the body of the report. A feasibility study dealing with a new electrical switching device prepared for a project committee consisting of electrical engineers would find this style appropriate.

DOCUMENTATION OF DATA

Data used in the feasibility study should be carefully documented as to source, manipulations performed on the data, and missing or incomplete data. This permits the reader to be fully informed about how data was obtained and used in the study. The logic of what was done and why should be easily followed by the reader.

There are two basic sources of data: primary and secondary. *Primary data* is data collected specifically for the feasibility study by the persons responsible for the study or their agents.

Secondary data is data which has already been collected and is available to the persons preparing the feasibility study. An example of secondary data is census data collected by the Census Bureau. This data is available at most large public libraries. When secondary data is used, sources and dates should be given along with special notes that help the reader understand the data. Of course, if a report is internal and company data is used, this clarification of data sources may not be necessary.

When primary data is collected for the study, the methodology used in the data collection process should be adequately described. The most appropriate place to put this description is in an appendix to the report. Such factors as sampling techniques, sample size, data collection technique, methods of analysis, and so on should be described in detail. Again, the reader should be able to understand how data was collected and used in the feasibility study.

Manipulation of data, such as averaging, deflating, and extrapolating should be explained in the body of the report or in notes accompanying any tables presented in the report. If data is missing for some year or only partial data is available, a note should be used to explain to the reader the circumstances of that data.

SUMMARY

Preparing a good written report of the results of the feasibility study is essential for effective communication of the results. How well the results are presented can often determine the acceptance or rejection of a project. The approach outlined in this chapter permits a clear, concise presentation which focuses on the major questions the readers would have in the results of the report.

Appendix B contains three feasibility studies prepared by the authors which implement the concepts presented in this book. These are all actual studies and represent some variety in subject matter and presentation formats. The names of people, places, and figures have been altered for anonymity.

APPENDIX A:
SOURCES OF
PUBLISHED
DATA

SOURCES OF CONSUMER DATA

Census of the Population (Government Printing Office). Taken every ten years, this source reports the population by geographic region, with detailed breakdowns according to demographic characteristics such as sex, marital status, age, education, race, income, and so on.

Consumer Market and Magazine Report Published annually by Daniel Starch, this source describes the household population of the U.S. with respect to a number of demographic variables and consumption statistics. The profiles are based on a large probability sample, and they give good consumer behavioral and socioeconomic characteristics.

Guide to Consumer Markets Published annually by Conference Board, this source provides data on the behavior of consumers, under the headings of population, employment, income, expenditures, production and distribution, and prices.

Historical Statistics of the U.S. from Colonial Times to 1957 This volume was prepared as a supplement to the *Statistical Abstract*. This source provides data on social, economic, and political aspects of life in the U.S. It contains consistent definitions and thus eliminates incompatabilities of data in the *Statistical Abstracts* caused by dynamic changes over time.

Marketing Information Guide Published monthly by the Department of Commerce, this source lists recently published studies and statistics that serve as a useful source of current information to marketing researchers.

COMPETITIVE DATA SOURCES

Almanac of Business and Industrial Ratios Published annually by Prentice-Hall, Inc., this source lists a number of businesses, sales, and certain operating ratios for several industries. The computations are from tax returns, supplied by the IRS, and the data allow comparison of a company's financial ratios with competitors of similar size.

Directory of Corporate Affiliations Published annually by National Register Publishing Company, Inc., this source lists approximately 3000 parent companies and their 16,000 divisions, subsidiaries, and affiliates.

Directory of Intercorporate Ownership Published in 1974 by Simon and Schuster, Volume 1 contains parent companies with their divisions, subsidiaries, overseas subsidiaries, and American companies owned by foreign firms. Volume 2 provides an alphabetical listing of all the entries in Volume 1.

Fortune Directory Published annually by *Fortune* magazine, this source presents information on sales, assets, profits, invested capital, and employees for the 500 largest U.S. industrial corporations.

Fortune Double 500 Directory Published annually in the May-August issues of *Fortune* magazine, this source offers information on assets, sales, and profits of 1000 of the largest U.S. firms, 50 largest banks, life insurance companies, and retailing, transportation, utility, and financial companies. In addition, this source ranks foreign firms and banks.

Middle Market Directory Published annually by Dun & Bradstreet, this source lists companies with assets in the range of $500,000 to $999,999. The directory offers information on some 30,000 companies' officers, products, sales, and number of employees.

Million Dollar Directory Published annually by Dun & Bradstreet, this source offers the same information as the *Middle Market Directory,* but only for companies with assets over $1 million.

Moody's Industrial Manual Published annually, this source provides information on selected companies products and description, history, mergers and acquisition record, principal plants and properties, principal offices, as well as seven years of financial statements and statistical records.

Moody's Manual of Investments This source documents historical and operational data on selected firms and five years of their balance sheets, income accounts, and dividend records.

Moody's Manuals This source lists includes manuals entitled *Banks and Finance, Municipals and Governments, Public Utilities, Transporation.* These manuals contain balance sheets and income statements for various companies and government units.

Reference Book of Corporate Managements Published annually by Dun & Bradstreet, this source lists 2,400 companies and their 30,000 officers and directors.

Sheldon's Retail Directory of the United States and Canada Published annually by Phelon, Sheldon & Marsar, Inc., this source supplies the largest chain, department, and specialty stores, by state and city and by Canadian province and city. This source also includes merchandise managers and buyers.

Standard and Poor's Register of Corporations, Directors and Executives Published annually by Standard and Poor, this source provides officers, sales, products, and number of employees for 30,000 U.S. and Canadian corporations.

State Manufacturing Directories Published for each state, these sources give company addresses, products, officers, and so on, by geographic location.

Thomas Register of American Manufacturers Published annually by the Thomas Publishing Company, this source gives specific manufacturers of individual products, as well as the company's address, branch offices, and subsidiaries.

Wall Street Journal Index Published monthly, this source lists corporate news, alphabetically, by firm name, as it has occurred in the Wall Street Journal.

MARKET DATA SOURCES

American Statistics Index: A Comprehensive Guide and Index to the Statistical Publications of the U.S. Government Published monthly by the Congressional Information Service, this source indexes statistical publications of federal agencies, and it is a useful starting point for obtaining market data.

Ayer Directory of Publications. Published annually by Ayer Press, this source is a comprehensive listing of newspapers, magazines, and trade publications of the United States (by states), Canada, Bermuda, Republics of Panama and the Phillippines, and the Bahamas.

Bureau of the Census Catalog (Government Printing Office). Published quarterly, this source is a comprehensive guide to Census Bureau publications. Publications include agriculture, foreign trade, governments, population and the economic census.

Business Conditions Digest (Government Printing Office). Bureau of Economic Analysis, Department of Commerce. Published monthly, this source gives indications of business activity in table and chart form.

Business Cycle Developments (Government Printing Office). Bureau of the Census. Published monthly, this source provides some 70 business activity indicators, that give keys to general economic conditions.

Business Periodicals Index. This source lists articles by subject heading from 150 or more business periodicals. It also suggests alternate key words which can be used to determine a standard of relevance in environmental analysis.

Business Statistics Department of Commerce. Published biennially, this source is a supplement to *Survey of Current Business.* It provides information from some 2,500 statistical series, starting in 1939.

Census of Business (Government Printing Office). Published every five years, this source supplies statistics on the retail, wholesale and service trades. The census of service trade compiles information on receipts, legal form of organization, employment and number of units by geographic area.

Census of Housing (Government Printing Office). Published every ten years, this source provides information on types of structures, size, condition, occupancy, monthly rent, average value, and equipment contained, by city blocks.

Census of Manufacturer (Government Printing Office). Published every five years, this source presents manufacturers by type of industry. It contains detailed industry and geographic statistics, such as the number of establishments, quantity of output, value added in manufacture, employment, wages, inventories, sales by customer class, and fuel, water, and energy consumption.

Census of Population (Government Printing Office). Taken every ten years, this source reports the population by geographic region, with detailed breakdowns according to demographic characteristics such as sex, marital status, age, education, race, national origin, family size, employment, and income.

Census of Retail Trade (Government Printing Office). Taken every five years in the years ending in 2 and 7, this source provides information on 100 retail classifications arranged by SIC numbers. Statistics are compiled on number of establishments, total sales, sales by product line, size of firms, employment and payroll for states, SMSA's, counties and cities of 2,500 or more.

Census of Selected Service Industries (Government Printing Office). Taken every five years, in years ending in 2 and 7, this source compiles statistics on 150 or more service classifications. Information on the number of establishments, receipts, payrolls, etc. are provided for various service organizations.

Census of Transportation (Government Printing Office). Taken every five years, in years ending in 2 and 7, this source presents three specific surveys: Truck Inventory and Use Survey, National Travel Survey, and Commodity Transportation Survey.

Census of Wholesale Trade (Government Printing Office). Taken every five years, in years ending in 2 and 7, this source provides statistics of 188 wholesale classifications. Information includes numbers of establishments, sales, personnel, payroll, and the like.

Commodity Yearbook Published annually by the Commodity Research Bureau, this source supplies data on prices, production, exports, stocks, and the like for 100 commodities.

County and City Data Book (Government Printing Office, 1972). Bureau of the Census. This publication gives statistics on population, income, education, employment, housing, retail and wholesales for various cities, SMSA's and counties.

County Business Patterns Departments of Commerce and Health, Education and Welfare. Published annually, this source gives statistics on the number of businesses by type and their employment and payroll broken down by county,.

Directory of Federal Statistics for Local Areas: A Guide to Sources (Government Printing Office). Published in 1966, this source looks at topics such as population, finance, income, education, and the like in a local perspective.

Directory of Federal Statistics for States: A Guide to Sources (Government Printing Office). Bureau of the Census. This source looks at topics such as population, finance, income, education and the like at the state level.

Economic Almanac Published every two years by the National Industrial Conference Board, this source gives data on population, prices, communications, transportation, electric and gas consumption, construction, mining and manufacturing output, in the United States, Canada, and other selected world areas.

Economic Indicators (Government Printing Office). Council of Economic Advisos, Department of Commerce. Published monthly, this source gives current key indicators of general business conditions, such as GNP, personal consumption expenditures, and the like.

Fand S. Index This detailed index on business-related subjects offers information about companies, industries, and products from numerous business-oriented newspapers, trade journals, financial publications, and special reports.

Federal Reserve Bulletin (Washington, D.C.: Federal Reserve System Board of Governors). Published monthly, this publication offers financial data on interest rates, credit, savings, banking activity; an index of industrial production; and finance and international trade statistics.

Handbook of Economic Statistics Economics Statistics Bureau. Published annually, this source presents current and historical statistics of United States industry, commerce, agriculture, and labor.

Market Analysis: A Handbook of Current Data Sources Written by Nathalie Frank and published by Scarecrow Press of Metuchen, N.J., 1969, this book offers sources of secondary information broken down on the basis of indexes, abstracts, directories, and the like.

Market Guide (New York: Editor and Publisher magazine). Published annually, this source presents data on population, principle industries, climate, transportation facilities, households, banks, and retail sales and outlets for 1500 newspaper markets in the United States and Canada.

Measuring Markets: A Guide to the Use of Federal and State Statistical Data (Government Printing Office). This publication lists federal and state publications covering population, income, employment, taxes, and sales. It is a useful starting point for the marketing researcher who is interested in locating secondary data.

Merchandising. Published annually in the March issue of this magazine is the "Statistical and Marketing Report," which presents charts and tables of sales, shipments, product saturation, and replacement, trade in, and import/export figures for home electronics, major appliances, and housewares. Also appearing annually in the May issue is the "Satistical and Marketing Forecast." This gives manufacturer's sales projections for the coming year and is useful in forecasting certain market factors.

Monthly Labor Review (Government Printing Office) Bureau of Labor Satistics. Published monthly, this source compiles trends and information on employment, wages, weekly working hours, collective agreements, industrial accidents, and wholesale and retail prices.

Predicasts (Cleveland, OH: Predicasts, Inc.) This abstract gives forecasts and market data, condensed to one line, from business and financial publications, trade journals and newspapers. It includes information on products, industries and the economy, and it presents a consensus forecast through 1985 for each data series.

Public Affairs Information Services Bulletin (PAIS) Similar to, but different from, the *Business Periodicals Index,* this source includes more foreign publications, and it includes many books, government publications, and many nonperiodical publications.

Rand McNally Commercial Atlas and Marketing Guide (Chicago: Rand McNally Company). Published annually, this source contains marketing data and maps for some 100,000 cities and towns in the United States. It includes such things as population, auto registrations, basic trading areas, manufacturing, transportation, population, and related data.

Reader's Guide to Periodical Literature This index presents articles from magazines of a general nature, such as *U.S. News and World Report, Time, Newsweek, Saturday Review.* It also suggests alternate key words that provide initial insight into the nature of the environment.

Sales Management Survey of Buying Power Published annually by Sales Management Magazine, this source provides information such as population, income, retail sales, and the like, broken down by state, county and SMSA, for the United States and Canada.

Standard and Poor's Industry Survey Published annually, this source offers current surveys of industries and a monthly Trends and Projections section, useful in forecasting market factors.

Standard and Poor's Trade and Securities Statistics Published monthly by Standard and Poor's, Corp., this source contains statistics on banking, production, labor, commodity prices, income, trade, securities, and the like.

Statistical Abstract of the United States (Government Printing Office). Bureau of the Census. Published annually, this source serves as a good initial reference for other secondary data sources. It includes data tables covering social, economic, industrial, political and demographic subjects.

Statistics of Income Internal Revenue Service. Published annually, this source gives balance sheet and income statement statistics, prepared from federal income tax returns of corporations, and broken down by major industry, asset size, and the like.

Survey of Buying Power Published annually by Sales Management, Inc., New York, this source gives information on population, income, and retail sales for each county and city of 10,000 population, or greater, in the United States, Canada, and Mexico.

Survey of Current Business (Government Printing Office). Bureau of Economic Analysis, Department of Commerce. Published monthly, this source presents indicators of general business, personal consumption expenditures, industry statistics, domestic trade, earnings and employment by industry, real estate activity, and the like.

U.S. Industrial Outlook (Government Printing Office). Published annually, this source provides a detailed analysis of approximately 200 manufacturing and nonmanufacturing industries. It contains information on recent developments, current trends, and a ten-year outlook for the industries. This source is useful in forecasting the specific marketing factors of a market analysis.

Wall Street Journal Index Published monthly, this source lists general news by subject as it has occurred in this business paper.

COST DATA SOURCES

Business Publication Rates and Data Published by Standard Rate & Data Service, Inc. This index lists trade publication sources.

Economic Census (United States' Government Printing Office). A comprehensive and periodic canvas of the United States' industrial and business activites, taken by the Census Bureau every five years. In addition to providing the framework for forecasting and planning, these censuses provide weights and benchmarks for indexes of industrial production, productivity, and price. Management uses these in economic or sales forecasting; analyzing sales performance; allocating advertising budgets; locating plants, warehouses and stores, and the like.

1977 Census of Manufacturers (Government Printing Office). This census of manufacturers in the United States provides statistics for each state, SCSA, SMSA, county, and selected cities. It includes employment, payrolls, inventories capital expenditures assets, retirements rental payments, depreciation, value added, and the like.

1977 Census of Manufacturers "Special Tabulations" of data from this source are available in summary form on a cost basis. It contains confidential information including individual business establishments. Inquiries should be directed to the Chief, Industry Division, Bureau of the Census, Washington, D.C., 20233.

Annual Survey of Manufacturers (Government Printing Office). Based on a sample of 70,000 it collects industry statistics normally requested by Census of Manufacturers, however, includes more detailed information on assets, capital expenditures, retirements, depreciation, supplemental labor costs and costs of purchased services on an annual basis.

Encyclopedia of Association Published by Gale Research Co. 1972. This source may acquaint a researcher with various associations for cost data pertaining to desired insutry.

Moody's Investors Services, Inc. Published by Standard & Poor Corporation (NY). A financial reporting source about many large firms.

Standard Corporation Records Published by Standard and Poor Corporation (NY). A publication of financial reporting data of the larger firms.

TRADE JOURNALS

Two examples of trade journals are shown below.

CREST Report (Chain Restaurant Eating Out Share Trends). Quarterly Supplement to Food Service Trends, published by the National Restaurant Association. The survey is designed to track expenditures and behavior in the commercial segment of the food service industry.

Food Service Trends Published by National Restaurant Association. For example, Wholesale Food Price Index and its percentage change is given for Farm Products, Processed Foods and Feeds on page 10 of the June 1979 Food Service Trends publication of the National Restaurant Association.

APPENDIX B:
THREE SAMPLE
FEASIBILITY
STUDIES

FEASIBILITY STUDY

BLUERIDGE PACKING COMPANY

Anytown, U.S.A.

Prepared by

Robert E. Stevens, Ph.D.
Philip K. Sherwood, Ed.D.

STEVENS-SHERWOOD AND ASSOCIATES
2140 S. 78th E. Ave.
Tulsa, Oklahoma

CERTIFICATION

We hereby certify that we have no interest, present or contemplated, in the proposed Blueridge Packing Company and that to the best of our knowledge and belief, the statements and information contained in this report are correct—subject to the limitations herein set forth.

_____

Robert E. Stevens, Ph.D.

_____

Philip K. Sherwood, Ed.D.

TABLE OF CONTENTS

EXECUTIVE SUMMARY

There are four major considerations in assessing the economic feasibility of the proposed Blueridge Packing Company.

Is there sufficient demand for beef and pork products in the three state market area to justify the establishment of an additional slaughtering operation?

An analysis of the population and consumption patterns for the three-state area compared to total output of present slaughtering operations in this three-state area shows a net excess of consumption when stated in animal equivalents of 1,477,400 cattle and 1,899,000 hogs. Projections of future demand indicate a further increase in the consumption of both beef and pork products for the market area. Therefore, it is concluded that there would be ample demand for the output of the proposed facility operating at the level of production of 75,000 hogs and 75,000 cattle annually.

Is there a sufficient supply of animals in the area of the proposed facility to support the proposed level of output of 75,000 cattle and 75,000 hogs annually?

Although there is a large inventory of cattle and hogs in the three-state area, the number of cattle available for slaughter is considerably lower than the inventory would indicate. The absence of feedlot operations in the area would necessitate the importation of approximately 20 percent of the cattle output of the facility. This would be approximately 15,000 cattle of the higher grades. With the present marketings of animals within the area and the proposed sales facility at Anytown, U.S.A., it is probable that the 60,000 cattle of lower grades could be acquired within the immediate area. Enough hogs to support the proposed level of operation of the plant are available in the market area.

> Can the proposed facility operate at a profit with the current market prices for beef and pork carcassed, proposed level of output, and the investment necessary to establish the proposed facility?

Annual revenues from the sale of carcasses and offal would total $30,074,450. Annual expenses for this level of production would total $29,005,894. The proposed facility could therefore operate at an annual net profit of $560,992 after taxes. These figures reflect average 1981 prices for animal inputs and carcasses.

> Will the profit realized from the operation of the proposed facility justify the investment?

The rate of return (investment divided by net profit) on the capital requirements of the $4,627,384 for the proposed operation would be only 12.12 percent. Using the excess present value technique to compare the present value of the returns (net profit plus depreciation) which can be expected over the life of the proposed facility with the capital requirements for establishing the proposed venture, it is concluded that the proposed venture is economically feasible. The annual cash flows produce a return in excess of 15 percent.

CHAPTER I

INTRODUCTION

Purpose

The purpose of this study was to determine the economic feasibility of a "kill and chill" operation to be located in Anytown, U.S.A. The study focused on the monetary feasibility of such an operation. This involved a preliminary assessment of markets for outputs and inputs of the proposed operation, projections of revenues and operating costs, and analysis of the anticipated return on investment.

Preliminary Assumptions

Several basic assumptions were made in developing the substantive materials which were analyzed in reaching the conclusions stated in the last section of the report.

Because of the anticipated size of the operation, it was assumed that the plant would be federally inspected so that sales could be made in interstate commerce. Inspection is performed by the Meat Inspection Division of the Agricultural Research Service of the U.S. Department of Agriculture. All meat which moves in interstate commerce must be federally inspected.[1]

---

[1]U.S. Inspected Meat Packing Plants, Agricultural Handbook No. 191, Agricultural Research Services, U.S. Department of Agriculture, Washington, D.C.

Second, it was assumed that the proposed plant would concentrate on the market area represented by the three states. The market potential existing in these states and the anticipated size of the operation warrant such an assumption as will be shown in the report.

The third assumption dealt with the exact nature of the operation. It was assumed that the plant would not be an integrated operation. That is, no feedlot operations would be maintained (other than that necessary to service working inventory) and no additional processing of slaughtered animals would take place. This assumption is based on information provided by the originators of the project and is vital in determining both costs and revenues to be derived from the proposed operation.

A final assumption was that the plant would operate at a predetermined level and sell its entire output. Certain basic facilities are required to start such an operation. However, the utilization of such equipment may vary considerably due to seasonal variations in the availability of cattle and hogs and changes in the market for the products of the firm. This specified level of operation would entail slaughtering an average of three hundred cattle and three hundred hogs daily. Using a 250 work day calendar, this would result in an annual slaughter of 75,000 cattle and 75,000 hogs or a 150,000 annual slaughter. (The average output of such plants is 18,000 heads annually.)[2] This production and sales level is vital to the analysis to follow. Operating at some other level of output than the one specified would substantially influence cost and revenues and would not be reflected in the analysis presented in this report.

---

[2]Product Identifications #3, Research and Development Center, Jackson, Mississippi, March, 1973.

It should also be pointed out that no attempt was made to analyze the managerial abilities of administrative personnel of the proposed plant. This was beyond the scope of this particular study. However, the profitability of any business operation is dependent on the possession of adequate managerial abilities by those personnel responsible for the decision making within the organization.

Other assumptions are noted in the report where they are needed to facilitate the analysis.

CHAPTER II

MARKET POTENTIAL FOR BEEF AND PORK

<u>Consumer Demand</u>

Per capita consumption of beef in the United States is an all-time high—116 pounds. This figure represents an increase of six pounds per capita in the seven-year period from 1965 to 1972. It is anticipated that consumption may reach 150 pounds per capita by 1982.[3]

The consumption of pork has also been increasing. Comparable figures are 63 pounds per capita in 1960, 67 pounds in 1972, and an anticipated 70 pounds per capita in 1985.[4]

Tables 1 and 2 combine population figures for the market area—the three market area states—with per capita consumption values to yield total consumption of beef and pork respectively. These values are then converted into the equivalent number of beef cows and hogs required to meet the consumption levels. These tables therefore show the number of beef cows and hogs consumed in the market area in 1980.

Market potential is defined as the maximum capacity of a market to purchase a specific type of offering in a specified time period. As shown in these two tables, consumption in the three-state area represents

---

[3]<u>The Farm Index</u>, Agricultural Research Service, U.S. Department of Agriculture, April, 1979.

[4]<u>Ibid</u>.

94

TABLE 1

ESTIMATED MARKET AREA BEEF CONSUMPTION FOR 1980

State	Population[a]	Per Capita[b] Beef Consumption (Pounds)	Total Beef Consumption (Pounds)	Beef Cow[c] Equivalents (1000 head)
State 1	3,521,600	116	408,505,600	756.5
State 2	3,733,600	116	433,097,600	802.0
State 3	2,269,500	116	263,262,000	487.5
	9,524,700		1,104,865,200	2,046.0

a. "Annual Survey of Buying Power," Sales Management, August, 1979.

b. The Farm Index, loc. cit.

c. Equivalent number of beef cows in thousands was computed using a 60 percent conversion factor and an average liveweight of 900 pounds.

considerable market potential. The equivalent of over two million beef cows and four million hogs were consumed in this three-state area in 1980. These calculations are based on 1980 population and consumption estimates, and it should be noted that this is a conservative estimate of potential for the proposed plant. By the time the plant would begin operations, there would have been an increase in both population and average consumption of beef and pork.

Availability of Livestock Supplies

The proposed plant will probably be unable to secure adequate supplies of livestock from within the market area. In fact, a recent publication of the Research and Development Center in Baytown states that about 50 percent of all animals slaughtered in State 3 came from other

TABLE 2

ESTIMATED MARKET AREA PORK CONSUMPTION FOR 1980

State	Population[a]	Per Capita[b] Pork Consumption (Pounds)	Total Pork Consumption (Pounds)	Hog[c] Equivalents (1000 head)
State 1	3,521,600	67	235,947,200	1,616.8
State 2	3,733,600	67	250,151,100	1,713.4
State 3	2,269,500	67	152,056,500	1,041.5
Totals	9,524,700		638,154,800	4,371.7

a. "Annual Survey of Buying Power," Sales Management, August 1979.

b. The Farm Index, loc. cit.

c. Equivalent number of hogs in thousands was computed using a 70 percent conversion factor and an average liveweight of 208 pounds.

states.[5] Table 3 shows the inventory of cattle and hogs in the market area in 1980.

Although the marketing of cattle and calves exceed slaughter in the market area, most of the marketings are calves which are shipped to large feedlots in the West. The relatively large inventory of cattle and hogs is thus somewhat misleading. Since it is more economical to ship calves out West and feed them than to ship feed into the market area, the number of cattle available for slaughter is substantially less than the inventory would indicate. The same situation is generally true of hogs. This lack of slaughter animals in the market area can be shown more clearly in Table 4. This table shows consumption and slaughter of cattle and hogs in the three-state area and the imports of animals needed to meet consumption levels.

TABLE 3
INVENTORY OF CATTLE AND HOGS IN STATE 1,
STATE 2, and STATE 3, 1980
(1000 head)

State	Cattle	Hogs
State 1	2,050	1,099
State 2	1,907	295
State 3	2,613	600
Totals	6,570	1,994

[5]Product Identification #3, Research and Development Center, Baytown, U.S.A., March, 1980.

TABLE 4

CONSUMPTION, SLAUGHTER, AND IMPORTS OF BEEF AND
PORK IN STATE 1, STATE 2, AND STATE 3, 1980
(1000 head)

State	Consumption[a]	Total[b] Slaughter	Imports
		Beef	
State 1	756.5	100.4	656.1
State 2	802.0	186.7	615.3
State 3	487.5	281.5	206.0
Totals	2,046.0	568.6	1,477.4
		Pork	
State 1	1,616.8	955.5	661.3
State 2	1,713.4	232.2	1,481.2
State 3	1,041.5	1,285.0	−243.5[c]
Totals	4,371.7	2,472.7	1,899.0

a. 100 head equivalents

b. Slaughter figures based on statistics in <u>Meat Animals</u>, April, 1973, loc. cit. and estimates based on 1980 farm slaughter values.

c. Slaughter of Pork exceeded consumption in State 3.

The equivalent of 1,477,400 beef cows and 1,899,000 hogs had to be imported into the three-state area to satisfy consumption needs in 1980.

Thus far, two basic facts have been established: (1) the excess of consumption over slaughter in the market area establishes the existence of adequate potential for another slaughtering operation in the area; and (2) the large amount of beef imported into the area to satisfy market demands indicates that only a portion of the slaughter animals for the proposed plant could be supplied from within the area. The additional supplies (higher grades of animals) would have to be purchased outside the market area and shipped in at higher prices.

The excess of hog slaughter over consumption in the state indicates that supplies of hogs in the area would probably be sufficient to support the anticipated levels of production.

For purposes of this study, it was assumed that 20 percent of the beef slaughter animals would come from outside the market area.

Market Prices—Animal Inputs

One of the major factors determining the profitability of the proposed operation is the cost of raw materials—cattle and hogs. For purposes of analysis, it was assumed that 20 percent of the cattle slaughtered by the plant would come from outside the market area. This assumption is based on the results of the analysis of the availability of animals previously discussed. At the proposed slaughter level of 75,000 cattle annually, this would mean that 15,0000 slaughter animals would have to be procured from outside the market area and 60,000 from within the area. All of the hogs slaughtered would be supplied from within the local area.

Even though the market for cattle and hogs was in such a state of uncertainty during the time period of the study, it was felt that a reasonable approach to determining prices of inputs and outputs was taken. Although these prices may change substantially by the time the actual operations begin, the margin of difference between the sets of prices should remain fairly constant.

The average price per hundredweight of beef cattle and hogs was $34.52 and $25.10 respectively for the United States in 1980. The average price for cattle and hogs in State 3 was $32.42 and $25.60 for the same period.[6]

In this study, the prices of $34.52 per hundredweight for beef cows from outside the area and $32.42 for those obtained within the area were used in computations. The hog price of $25.60 per hundredweight was used as the relevant hog input price. The difference in prices for beef inputs seems reasonable since the beef obtained outside the area would be higher grade animals.

There would also be a difference in transportation cost for animals obtained from outside the market area. Interviews with local truck operators and packing companies indicate that the rates for transportation of livestock is in a state of change toward higher rates and a difference in methods used in computing rate. Both will cause higher transportation costs in the future.

In computing transportation cost, a rate of $.60 per hundredweight was used for animals acquired within the market area and $.90 per hundredweight for animals brought in from outside the market area.

---

[6]Agricultural Prices: 1980 Annual Summary, USDA, June, 1981.

CHAPTER III
COST OF THE FACILITY

Land Costs

The proposed slaughtering facility is to be located ten miles south of Anytown, U.S.A., on State 3 Highway 7; 54 miles southeast of Baytown; 34 miles north of Saytown; 124 miles from New Cravens; and 43 miles from Tunis. This location places the proposed facility in an area which is relatively central to the major population concentration in the market area. This area also seems to have an adequate labor supply, is a major livestock producing area, and has relatively low land values for industrial development of $1,951 per acre. While this figure is somewhat higher than average land prices of $750–$1,000 per acre for similar land around Anytown, it is considerably lower than comparable land nearer major population areas and the appraised value of the land.[7]

One hundred acres have been acquired by the corporation in exchange for stock. The total cost for this land is $195,100. Immediate space requirements for the plant facility, holding pens sufficient for at least 600 cattle and 600 hogs, parking lots and truck loading docks, water well sites, adequate expansion space, and sewage treatment facilities would not exceed fifteen acres.

---

[7] Appraisal by Bob E. Jones, real estate appraiser, Anytown, 1980. Average cost/acre figures from B. L. Smith, real estate appraiser, Anytown.

One hundred acres is thus far in excess of the actual space requirement needs and the expenditure for this amount substantially influences the rate of return on investment.

Conversely, there are several possible arguments in favor of initial acquisition of the total acreage. Firstly, it provides the company with control of the environment in which the plant is located. This would enable the company to undertake future expansion into auxillary processing operations or vertical integration of a feeding operation should economic conditions warrant. Secondly, once the proposed plant is in operation, land adjacent to it would increase in value above the present costs. And finally, any additional industrial development could be controlled by the company and would be an important fact in encouraging related industry, as well as becoming an additional source of revenue for the company. No attempt was made to judge the relative merits of these arguments.

Building Costs

Table 5 shows the breakdown of building costs for the proposed facility. These cost estimates were provided by Kohe Supplies, Inc., Kansas City, Kansas. Although architectural specifications would be necessary for an accurate estimate of building costs, these estimates at an average of $32.40 seem to be somewhat high. Local estimates supplied by the originators of the project were approximately $20 per square foot. It is assumed that the local estimate includes the special building character-istics required of a federally inspected slaughter facility. The local estimate is an average figure for the total building with the processing areas higher and nonprocessing areas at a much lower rate. Using local estimates, the cost of the plant facility would be $635,080.

TABLE 5

BREAKDOWN OF BUILDING COSTS*

Work Area	Square Feet	Cost Per Square Foot	Cost
Basement	9,072	$30.00	$ 272,160
Kill Floor	9,072	35.00	317,520
Beef Chill Cooler	2,560	35.00	89,600
Beef Holding Cooler	2,688	35.00	94,080
Hog Cooler	1,600	35.00	57,225
Edible Cooler	650	35.00	22,750
Cutting Room	2,304	32.00	73,728
Dry Storage Room	480	30.00	14,400
Shipping Dock	768	32.00	24,576
Office and Rest Rooms	2,560	25.00	64,000
Totals	31,754	32.40 (average)	$1,030,039

*See Appendix A.

The accuracy of the estimate of building costs will substantially influence the capital required to initiate the project. A variance of $1.00 per square foot would amount to a $31,754 error. Therefore, without architectural plans and a firm bid from a local contractor, it must be assumed that the estimate provided by Koch Supplies is the best present estimate available since it reflects the judgment of a firm experienced in the construction of slaughtering facilities. It is assumed that the present figures include allowances for parking and holding pens sufficient for 600 cattle and 600 hogs which is a two-day supply at the state level of output. According to federal regulations, holding pens must be paved with curbs. Parking areas must also be hard surface to keep airborne particles to an acceptable level. It is assumed that the local estimates do not include these features. Also, according to information supplied by the originators of the project, the Koch estimates include an additional 15 percent to offset possible increases in building materials and labor costs before the facility could be built. This would account for $154,505 of the discrepancy between the two estimates. The remaining $240,454 difference in estimates is an amount in excess of the possible costs of holding pens and parking facilities. It may be a reflection of the differences in labor costs for construction between Kansas City and Anytown. Verifying the accuracy of these estimates is beyond the scope of the present investigation and perhaps not possible without architectural plans which are not available. Therefore, the Koch estimates will be used in the financial and economic analysis as the best present estimate of the complete facility including building, holding pens, parking, and loading facilities.

Table 6 shows other building costs estimates supplied by Koch Supplies, Inc. Since the land required does not have existing water and sewage treatment facilities adequate to handle the needs of the proposed slaughtering facility, these costs are shown here. Again, these figures are 15 percent above present costs to offset effects of inflation before actual construction can be completed. This is $23,250 in excess of present costs.

TABLE 6
OTHER BUILDING COSTS*

Site Preparation	$ 25,000
Sewer System	50,000
Engineering	50,000
Road Work	30,000
Total	$155,000

*See Appendix A.

Federal regulations and practical considerations require that access roads in the vicinity of the plant be hard surface. Costs for drilling two 900 foot water wells and constructing a tank to meet the needs of the proposed facility of 30,000 gallons per hour are not included because of the lack of available data.

Equipment Costs

An itemized listing and current prices of equipment necessary to outfit the proposed facility is included in Appendix B. Total equipment costs f.o.b. Koch Supplies, Inc., Kansas City, Kansas, are $829,457. It is assumed that the equipment listed and the prices quoted are in competition with industry rates and that the equipment is adequate for the type of operation and the proposed level of output of the facility. Transportation of equipment to the plant site and installation are not included in these figures.

Average industry transportation costs are five percent of sales price and installation costs are 17 percent of sales price. Again, the equipment prices are 15 above current prices to offset future price increases before the plant can be completed. For the purposes of this report, the 15 percent will be used to partially offset transportation and installation charges. Should price increases occur before the plant is constructed, it is possible that total costs for equipment, installation, and transportation to the plant site would be considerably higher than the total shown here.

All fixed cost estimates supplied by Koch Supplies, Inc. are 15 percent above current costs. This is a total of $177,756.

In addition, the difference between costs estimates of the building from Koch and local contractors is $354,959. This would provide $532,716 to cover construction of holding pens, water supply, transportation, and installation of equipment, architectural fees, and parking areas. Assuming a certain amount of inaccuracy in the estimates of local contractors without firm bids or architectural specifications, it is probable that the costs estimates by Koch are sufficiently inflated to cover the non-specific items mentioned and retain a comfortable cushion for possible future price increases. The breakdown of costs estimates supplied by Koch is considered to be quite unrealistic in many instances, but the overall cost estimate of the facility and equipment is the highest possible cost assuming that the facility could be built for considerably less than these estimates. This would substantially reduce the capital investment and also affect estimates of the rate of return on investment. Table 7 summarizes the total costs of the facility.

Working Capital Requirements

The meat and processing industry is an industry requiring a large investment in working capital. Most of the working capital is used to finance the large inventories of slaughter animals. Recent financial records of two firms in the meat industry revealed a net working capital of about ten percent of sales. Initial working capital requirements would not be quite this large. It will be shown in Chapter IV that total yearly expenses of operations are estimated to be $29,013,471. Assuming that initial working capital requirements are equal to one month's expenses yields a requirement of $2,417,788. This seems to be a reasonable amount considering the methods of payment and factoring services available in the industry.

For purposes of this study, a $2,417,788 investment in working capital was assumed to be the appropriate capital needed to begin operations. This figure is about eight percent of the anticipated sales revenue.

TABLE 7
SUMMARY OF FACILITY COSTS

Source	Costs
Land	$ 195,100
Building	1,030,039
Other Building Costs	155,000
Equipment	829,457
Total	$2,209,596

Since the investment in building, land, and equipment totaled $2,209,596, the total capital requirements will be $4,627,384. Thus the proposed venture would be one of the largest undertaken in the state in recent years.

CHAPTER IV

REVENUES, EXPENSES, AND RETURN ON INVESTMENT

Revenues

The revenue derived from operations will come from two sources: (1) sales of the carcasses of the slaughtered animals and (2) sales of by-products of the slaughtered operation. As previously pointed out, there will be no processing of hogs into pork products such as bacon, sausage, and the like in the proposed operation. Thus, revenue will come basically from carcass sales and the sales of hides and offal of the slaughtered animals. Output of the plant will be sold primarily to other meat wholesalers and processors. Table 8 shows the sales revenues from the output of the operation.

Beef Sales Revenues

The average wholesale price of a beef carcass in 1980 was $53.87 per hundredweight.[8] The estimated average price for hides and offal of cattle was $4.18 per hundred pounds liveweight. Thus, a 900-pound slaughter animal would yield about $291 in carcass sales (5.4 hundred-weight [cut] times $53.87) and $38 in hide and offal revenue (9 hundred-weights times $4.18).

Total revenue for the 75,000 annual cattle slaughter would amount to $24,637,850—$21,816,350 in carcass revenues and $2,821,500 in revenues from the hides and offal.

---

[8]Livestock and Meat Situation, March, 1980, USDA, p. 22.

TABLE 8

SALES REVENUES BY PRODUCT TYPE

Product Type	Number of[a] Hundredweights of Each Product Produced	Sales Price per Hundredweight	Total Revenues By Product Type
Beef			
Carcass	405,000[c]	$53.87	$21,816,350
Hides and Offal	675,000[d]	4.18	2,821,500
Total Revenue—Beef			$24,637,850
Pork			
Carcass	156,000[c]	$30,28[e]	$ 4,723,680
Hides and Offal	156,000[d]	4.57[e]	712,920
Total Revenue—Pork			$ 5,436,600
Total Revenue—Beef and Pork			$30,074,450

a. Based on 75,000 cattle and 75,000 hogs slaughtered at an average liveweight of 900 and 208 pounds respectively. Conversion rates of 60 and 70 percent were used in completing the number of hundredweights of each product type.

b. Based on average prices per hundredweight of carcasses, hides, and offal for 1980.

c. Dressed weight for cattle and liveweight for hogs.

d. Liveweight—prices for offal and hides are reported in USDA publications in terms of estimates per hundredweight of live animals.

e. Estimated from industry revenue percentages for carcasses and by-products.

Pork Sales Revenues

The average wholesale value of pork, including by-products, was $34.85 per hundred pounds liveweight in 1980.[9] Since pork is usually processed into bacon, sausage, hams, and the like before being sold to retailers, the wholesale value of pork was used instead of the wholesale price. The difference in the wholesale value and the wholesale price should reflect the additional processing cost or value added by processing.

Pork by-products, including lard, would yield approximately $4.57 per hundredweight. Carcass value would average about $30.28 per hundred-weight. Total revenue from hog slaughter would amount to $5,436,600—$4,723,680 in carcass revenues and $712,920 in revenues from by-products.

The combined revenues for the proposed plant would be approximately $30,074,450 in 1980 prices.

Operating Expenses

Four major categories of expenses are discussed in this section: cost of animal inputs, wages and salaries, other employee expenses, and other operating expenses.

Cost of Animal Inputs

One of the major operating costs for the proposed plant will be the cost of animal inputs. Table 9 shows the breakdown of the cost of these inputs.

To derive the total cost of each input type, the following basic formula was used:

Total cost of the input = Number of animals X (average slaughter weight ÷ one hundred) X average price per hundredweight plus transportation per hundredweight X total hundredweights of animals.

---

[9]Livestock and Meat Statistics, USDA, 1980, p. 283.

TABLE 9
COST OF ANIMAL INPUTS

Inputs	Number[a] of Animals	Price per 100 lbs.	Total Cost
Cattle			
Within Market Area	60,000	$33.02	$17,830,000
Outside Market Area	15,000	35.42	4,781,700
Hogs	75,000	26.20	4,087,200
Totals	150,000		$26,698,900

a. Based on the assumption of a 75,000 annual cattle slaughter and 20 percent obtained outside the market area. Average slaughter weights of 900 lbs. and 208 lbs. were used for cattle and hogs respectively.

b. Prices include transportation costs of $.60/cwt within the area and $.90/cwt outside the area.

For the 60,000 cattle supplied through market area sources, a price of $32.42 per hundredweight and a transportation rate of $.60 was used. A price of $34.52 and a transportation rate of $.90 was used for the 15,000 cattle to be procured from outside the area. These calculations yielded a total cost of cattle inputs of $22,611,700. This was $17,830,000 for cattle procured in the area and $4,781,700 for animals outside the area.

For hogs, a price of $25.60 and a transportation rate of $.60 was used in calculations. This yielded a total cost of hogs inputs of $4,087,200 of the 75,000 annual slaughter. The combined cost of animal inputs totaled $26,698,900.

Wages and Salaries

The personnel for the plant totals 127. Of this total, 115 are production or auxillary personnel with 86 of these employees classified as unskilled and 29 as skilled. Information supplied by the U.S.A. Employment Security Division estimates the industry average wages for jobs classified as unskilled is $3.25 per hour and for skilled workers, $3.85. Appendix C gives the job titles, number of employees, and skill level. Total costs per year for production workers for fifty forty-hour weeks is $552,300.

Table 10 shows the office and administrative personnel and yearly salaries for each. Salaries of management personnel quoted are for personnel experienced in the slaughter industry. Total yearly salaries for office and administrative are $127,400. Total yearly wages and salaries for all personnel is $679,700.

TABLE 10
SALARY SCHEDULE FOR ADMINISTRATIVE AND OFFICE PERSONNEL

Position	Salary
Plant Manager	$ 31,000 (includes $1,000 expenses)
Production Manager	20,000
Sales Manager	17,000 (includes $1,000 expenses)
Personnel Manager	12,000
Receptionist	4,800
Office Workers (6)	30,600
Accountant	12,000
Total	$127,400

Other Employee Expenses

Other expenses of the proposed operation directly related to personnel are insurance and hospitalization; employment security taxes; social security taxes; vacation, holidays, and sick leave; and retirement.

The company's expense for an insurance and hospitalization program would be approximately $21,336. This is based on estimates supplied by a local insurance representative who quoted an industry average of $14.00 per employee. This figure includes average life insurance and hospitalization benefits for the local area. For all plant personnel, monthly premiums would total $1,778.

Employment security taxes vary with the claim record of the employer, however, the industry average for the local area is 2.5 percent of total wages and salaries. Assuming a normal employment pattern, the total employment security taxes would be $16,992.

Social security taxes are figured at the rate of 6.85 percent of the first $12,000 in earning. Using the average wage figures for production and auxiliary personnel, all of the total wages of $552,300 would be subject to social security taxes. Salaries of $95,400 for office and administrative personnel would be subject to social security taxes. Total employer's contribution for social security would be $37,890.

Paid vacation, holidays, and sick leave is figured at ten working days. Total costs would be $22,092. Since salaried personnel are paid on a monthly basis, this figure includes only the additional expenses for wage employees.

It is assumed that a company of this size will have a retirement program for its employees. Because a retirement plan has not been formulated by the originators of the project, the minimal contribution by the employer of such a program is taken as equal to the social security taxes. This is below the industry average; however, since State 3 corporations do not typically have retirement programs, it is considered adequate. Table 11 summarizes the expenses for wages, salaries, and employee benefits.

Other Expenses

In addition to the operation expenses previously estimated, several other categories of expenses should be identified and enumerated.

TABLE 11
TOTAL ANNUAL EMPLOYEE EXPENSE SCHEDULE

Item	Cost
Wages and Salaries:	
Production and Auxillary Personnel	$552,300
Administrative and Office Personnel	127,400
Employee Benefits:	
Insurance and Hospitalization	21,336
Employment Security Taxes	16,992
Social Security Taxes	37,890
Vacation, Holidays, and Sick Leave	22,092
Retirement	37,890
Total Expenses	$815,898

As was shown in Chapter III, the total investment required in the proposed operation would be about $4,628,000. Assuming all authorized stock is sold and $3,400,000 (value of authorized stock issue minus stock sales commissions and other fees) is available for financing the investment, an additional $1,228,000 would have to be secured through debt financing. The originators of the project plan to apply for an FHA-secured loan for the additional finances needed to begin operations. If this application is accepted, an 8.25 percent loan could be obtained.

Based on a repayment period of 25 years and an 8.25 percent interest rate, the debt retirement and interest schedule would be shown in Table 12. Total interest charges over the life the loan would be $1,317,016. This would be an average interest expense of $52,681.

TABLE 12
DEBT RETIREMENTS AND INTEREST SCHEDULE

Year	Principal	Annual Interest Charge	End of Year Payment
1	$1,228,000	$101,310	$49,120
2	1,178,880	97,258	49,120
3	1,129,760	93,205	49,120
4	1,080,640	89,153	49,120
5	1,031,520	85,100	49,120
6	982,400	81,048	49,120
7	933,280	76,943	49,120
8	884,160	72,943	49,120
9	835,040	68,891	49,120
10	785,920	64,838	49,120
11	736,800	60,786	49,120
12	687,680	56,733	49,120
13	638,560	52,681	49,120
14	589,440	48,628	49,120
15	540,320	44,576	49,120
16	491,200	40,524	49,120
17	442,080	36,471	49,120
18	392,960	32,419	49,120
19	343,840	28,366	49,120
20	294,720	24,314	49,120
21	245,600	20,262	49,120
22	196,480	16,209	49,120
23	147,360	12,157	49,120
24	98,240	8,105	49,120
25	49,120	4,052	49,120

The investment in equipment and building developed in Chapter III was $2,014,496: $829,457 for the equipment and $1,185,039 for the building. Assuming the equipment would be depreciated over an eight-year period and the building over a 25-year period, the annual depreciation expense would total $213,992.

The current millage for property taxes in Stevens County is 61 mills, and assessed values are about 15 percent of market values. Using this tax rate and structure, the annual property tax for the proposed plant would be $22,143.

The expense for supplies and containers averages about 2.1 percent of total sales. Since there will be no processing of slaughtered animals, a figure of 1 percent of sales was used for the plant. This would be about $300,745 a year. All other expenses are estimated at 3 percent of sales which is the industry average for regional meat packers.[10] This would be $902,233 in the proposed operation on an annual basis. This includes expenses for power, fuel, legal and audit charges, sales expenses, bad debt expense, and so on.

Pro Forma Income Statement

The previous sections of this chapter set forth the results of the analysis of anticipated revenues and expenses for the proposed venture. These results have been used to develop the pro forma income statement shown in Table 13. Expenses, including cost of animal inputs, totaled $29,005,894. This amount was subtracted from total sales revenue to determine profits before taxes. Federal and state corporate income taxes were then subtracted to determine the net profits from operations: $560,992.

Present Value Analysis and Return on Investment

The returns from an investment are defined for decision-making purposes as the net inflows of cash expected from a project.[11] In the case

[10]Financial Facts About the Meat Packing Industry, American Meat Institute, Chicago, Illinois, 1980, p. 9.

[11]Carl L. Moore and Robert K. Jaedicke, Managerial Accounting, Second Edition, Southwestern Publishing Company, Cincinnati, Ohio, 1967, p. 535.

TABLE 13
PRO FORMA INCOME STATEMENT

Sales		$30,074,450
Cost of Inputs		−26,698,900
Gross Margin		$ 3,375,550
Expenses	$679,700	
Salaries and Wages		
Other Employee Expenses:		
Insurance	21,336	
Retirement	37,890	
Vacation and Sick Leave	22,092	
Social Security Taxes	37,890	
Employment Security Taxes	16,992	
Other Expenses		
Depreciation	213,292	
Interest	52,681	
Property Taxes	22,143	
Supplies	300,745	
All Other Expenses	902,233	
Total Expenses		$ 2,306,994
Profit Before Income Taxes		$ 1,068,556
Corporate Income Taxes (Federal and State)		$− 507,564
Net Profit After Taxes		$ 560,992

of the proposed venture, this would be equal to the net profit after taxes plus depreciation: $774,284. The total capital requirements for the plant were computed to be $4,627,384. The weighted average life of the investment would be 18 years.

The excess present value is a common technique used to determine whether the returns from an investment justify the capital requirements of the investment.[12]

---

[12]Ibid., p. 53.

The present value of the returns over the life of the investment are equal to $5,744,812 ($774,284 X 6.128 at a 15 percent minimum acceptable rate of return). Since the present value of the returns ($4,744,812) is greater than the capital requirements ($4,627,384) of the project, the proposed venture is economically feasible.

The rate of return on investment is computed by dividing net profit after taxes by the total investment. The rate of return for the proposed operation is equal to 12.12 percent.

The rate of return does not consider net cash inflows generated by a project since it is computed using net profits. The net profit figure of $560,992 represents only a 1.86 percent return on sales. This return on sales reflects the low overall profitability of the meat industry.

CHAPTER V
CONCLUSIONS

This study was conducted within the framework of the assumptions stated throughout the first four chapters. The conclusions reached on the basis of this study are tenable only within the framework of these assumptions. For example, it was assumed that the level of output would be 150,000 slaughtered animals annually. If, in fact, a higher level of production could be achieved, net profit should be increased. On the other hand, a lower level of output should decrease net profits.

Based on the analysis of the return on investment and the present value of the cash flows generated by the investment, the plant is economically feasible. The present value of cash flows over the life of the investment was greater than the investment required to begin operations. Although net profits as a percent of sales are low, the rate of return on investment was estimated at 12.12 percent.

The reader should be cautioned that many of the figures used in this study were estimates based on projections of historical data collected specifically for this study. There is no way to determine the reliability of such estimates; however, these figures are the best estimates available.

APPENDIX A

BREAKDOWN OF BUILDING COSTS ESTIMATES

BLUERIDGE PACKING COMPANY

		Sq. Ft.	Cost Per Sq. Ft.	Cost
Basement	72 X 126	9072	$30.00	$ 272,160.00
Kill Floor	72 X 126	9072	35.00	317,520.00
Beef Chill Cooler	40 X 64	2560	35.00	89,600.00
Beef Holder Cooler	42 X 64	2688	35.00	94,080.00
Hog Cooler	32 X 50	1600	35.00	57,225.00
Edible Cooler	13 X 50	650	35.00	22,750.00
Cutting Room	48 X 48	2304	32.00	73,728.00
Dry Storage Room	12 X 40	480	30.00	14,400.00
Shipping Dock	64 X 12	768	32.00	24,576.00
Office and Rest Rooms	80 X 32	2560	25.00	64,000.00

Building Cost	$1,030,039.00
Equipment Cost	829,427.00
Site Preparation	25,000.00
Sewer System.	50,000.00
Engineering.	50,000.00
Road Work	30,000.00
Preliminary Total Estimate of Project	$2,014,496.00

APPENDIX B
ITEMIZED EQUIPMENT COST LIST

QUOTATION

Blueridge Packing Company
Anytown
U.S.A.

To the attention of: Robert E. Stevens

ITEM NO.	CAT. NO.	QUANTITY	DESCRIPTION	WEIGHT/CUBE APPROX.	PRICE EACH	TOTAL PRICE
1	1825	2	Cash Knocker		223.00	$450.00
2	1824	10M	Cartridges		M/38.50	385.00
3	7419	1	Revolving Knocking Pen Door			695.00
4	KOCH	1	10 gauge metal 3″ angle frame, air-operated entrance door			495.00
5	7403	1	7½ h.p. Hoist, magnetic starter, push button switch, limit switch			1650.00
6	7411	1	Automatic Lander, 30'0″ chain, limit switch			600.00
7	5302	1 Set	64'0″ bleeding ½″ X 3″ track, 4 offset cast iron hangers, 14″ drop, 5 double heel cast iron hangers, 14″ drop, 9 set I-Beam clips, 1 guide plate			947.00
8	2440	2	Blood and water drains, 4″ outlet		65.00	130.00
9	KOCH	1	Drop finger bleeding conveyor with 687 chain pusher, 8'0″ O.C. - 59'0″ active chain hangers 24″ O.C., 46'0″ idle chain			9500.00

ITEM NO.	CAT. NO.	QUANTITY	DESCRIPTION	WEIGHT/CUBE APPROX.	PRICE EACH	TOTAL PRICE
			hangers, 36″ O.C., 4 - 6-tooth bronze bushings, take-up, 1 worm gear, conveyor drive with 6-tooth shear pin hub, drive sprocket, 1 automatic air operated feeder to include hangers, I-Beam clip, double channels with bolts, guard rails with bolts and chains with pusher 5'0″ O.C.			
10	5302	1	Shackle return rail 48'0″ - $\frac{1}{2}$″ X $2\frac{1}{2}$″ track, 16 hangers and guard rail, 1 - 5'0″ shackle storage rail			497.00
11	7049	1	Shackle Lowerator			$550.00
12	7325 Spec	1	Electric Hydraulic Shackle Lowerator complete with 5 h.p. motor, starter and limit switches and push bottons			3120.00
13	KOCH	1	Drop rail No. 2 Transfer Section			120.00
14	KOCH	1	Drop Finger Skin Conveyor with 678 chain, pusher 5'0″ O.C., 98'0″ idle chain hangers 36″ O.C., 5 - 8-tooth bronze bush sprockets, 5 - 6-tooth bronze bush sprockets, 1 - 6-tooth bronze bush take-up, 1 worm gear conveyor drive with 6-tooth shear pin hub, drive sprocket, 5 sprocket carousels, 2 steel corners, 2 auto spreaders, with auto, controls and air combination unit, 2 spring switches -			

No.	Model	Qty.	Description	Unit Price	Amount
			also hangers, I-Beam clips, double channels with bolts, extra hangers and switches, guard rail with bolts and chain and pushers		14,950.00
15	7030 1-2-3-4	1	Koch-Johnson Hide Puller with Guide-A-Hide, Shear Pin Hub, Vari-Speed Drive and chain sterilizer, push botton switch		6275.00
16	7425	2	Air-operated galvanized elevator platform with all controls and combination units, extended base to match puller and knife sterilizer box	1050.00	2100.00
17	KOCH	1	5'0" stroke, 4" diameter air pusher with controls and combination unit and mount bracket		725.00
18	KOCH	1	Moving top viscera inspection table, 30'0" long, framework galvanized, galvanized sterilizer with vented hood, gear reducer, boot sterilizer with platform locker, one stainless steel retained viscera pan		16,950.00
19	KOCH	1	Variable speed drive for driving bleeding conveyor, skin conveyor and split conveyor and viscera table, to include variable speed transmission jack shaft, mitre gear box, roller chain drives, viscera table drive, 1200 rpm encapsulated motor, 15 h.p. with starter and push buttons		$12,000.00

ITEM NO.	CAT. NO.	QUANTITY	DESCRIPTION	WEIGHT/CUBE APPROX.	PRICE EACH	TOTAL PRICE
20	KOCH	1	Head and Tongue Conveyor 120'0" long with $\frac{3}{8}$" galvanied cable with double wheel trolleys and stainless steel head and tongue hooks, 3'0" O.C., also horizontal and vertical curves, take-up, galvanized hood sterilizer, variable speed drive, head and tongue plow, galvanized drip pans			11,250.00
21	KOCH	See Below	Platform, center pole construction, 4" dia. center pole 3" X 3" X $\frac{1}{4}$" angle frame, $1\frac{1}{2}$" guard rails, grip-strut floors, lavatory bases, all hot dip galvanized, as follows:			
22	KOCH	1	Hind Leg Platform, 4'0" X 3'0" wide, 26'0" long with ladder			2190.00
23	KOCH	3	14 gauge galvanized chutes, 2 legs, 1 udder		570.00	1410.00
24	KOCH	1	3'0" X 6'0" Rump Platform			495.00
25	KOCH	1	Rail and Head Inspection Platform, 3'0" X 8'0" long, 4 legs			797.00
26	KOCH	1	Final Inspection Platform, 4'0" X 3'0", 4 legs			427.00
27	7426	1	High and low wash Platform, 3'0" X 10'0"			1100.00
28	KOCH	1	High and low Shroud Platform			1100.00
29	KOCH	1	U-Shape Platform in front of Hide Puller			789.00

126

30	KOCH	Side Moving Splitting Platform, work surface 3'0" X 3'0" with all controls and saw suspension, galvanized	1	1250.00
31	7061	3-compartment Revolving Head Flusher with hose and valve	1	520.00
32	KOCH	Head Hatchet	1	29.00
33	7201	Paunch Table 8'0" stainless steel 14 gauge top, 8" gutter, with 4" drain safety pipe 7'0" manure box, $\frac{1}{2}$" spray valve, side platform and tripe umbrella of stainless steel and slides	1	$2750.00
34	7435	Tripe Scalder, stainless steel drum, galvanized frame, 2 h.p. motor, starter and thermometer	1	3410.00
35	77105	Tripe Inspection Ring, galvanized frame, stainless steel hook	1	155.00
36	2476	Pluck Table, stainless steel top, galvanized frame	1	520.00
37	7101 2041	Head Work Table, 8'0" stainless steel top, galvanized frame, Durasan board, $\frac{1}{2}$" spray valve	1	610.00
38	KOCH	Tongue wash truck, 26" X 42" plastic, galvanized frame	1	290.00
39	5302	Tracking 176'0" of $\frac{1}{2}$" X 2$\frac{1}{2}$" track, steel hangers, 13$\frac{1}{2}$" drop, 2-gear operated switches, conveyor switch, 1 gear-operated switch	1	590.00

ITEM NO.	CAT. NO.	QUANTITY	DESCRIPTION	WEIGHT/CUBE APPROX.	PRICE EACH	TOTAL PRICE
40	1213 1214	8	Jarvis Air Knives, with combination unit, hose and bracket		500.00	4000.00
41	KOCH	8 pr.	Extra blades		20.00	160.00
42	1227	2	Jarvis Hook Cutter with combination unit and hose		550.00	1100.00
43	BR-1	1	Jarvis Blade Grinder			1290.00
44	1217	1	Jarvis Scribe Saw and combination unit			420.00
45	2733	2	Splitting Saw B&D with starter		1300.00	2600.00
46	190-K	1	Saw Balancer			220.00
47	2745	1	Brisket Saw, B&D, with starter			690.00
48	50-J	1	Saw Balancer			$170.00
49	2725	1	Splitting Saw Sterilizer, galvanized			135.00
50	7126	1	Pan sterilizer, galvanized			140.00
51	1932 1932-555 1932-551	12	Sterilizing lavatories, stainless steel knife box, drinking fountain, foot valve, soap dispenser		175.00	2275.00
52	1933	1	Wall hung Lavatories with knife box, drinking fountain, foot valves and soap dispenser			240.00
53	7976	1	1000-lb. Budgit hoist with Container and 20'0" chain for trolleys and shrouds			427.00
54	KOCH	1	Plexiglas Saw shield			490.00

No.	Model	Qty	Description	Unit Price	Total
55	1930	4	Offal Hanging Trucks	400.00	1600.00
56	56289	2	Offal Pan Trucks with special drain gutters	790.00	1580.00
57	1925-HD	4	Heavy Duty trolley trucks	240.00	960.00
58	1924	8	Trolley Racks	55.00	440.00
59	KOCH	1	18 GPM Pump with 5 h.p. motor and 2 guns		1990.00
60	3633	6	Offal Drums with ring	37.00	222.00
61	KOCH	1	Koch-Fairbanks Overhead Track Scale for use with conveyorized track including Print-O-Matic attachment, weight only printed on tag		3990.00
62	KOCH	1	Shroud Tank, 30″ X 30″ X 30″ Goodyear Tank on galvanized frame		240.00
63	KOCH	1	Hide Chain Return Conveyor		950.00
64	1924	1	3-compartment Trolley Wash Tank with two steam controls		1040.00
65	5282	800	Trolleys, heat treated black frame, $\frac{5}{8}''$ X $6\frac{1}{2}''$ stainless steal hooks	4.95	3960.00
66	5299	15	Shackles with cast steel wheel and bronze bushings	42.00	$630.00
67	KOCH	4	Shroud storage truck, 25″ X 25″ X 25″ Goodyear tank and galvanized frame	320.00	1280.00
68	1727	2	Drum trucks, all steel construction	79.00	158.00
69	KOCH	1	Slide-out type stainless steel washer, with auto 2-way		12,500.00

ITEM NO.	CAT. NO.	QUANTITY	DESCRIPTION	WEIGHT/CUBE APPROX.	PRICE EACH	TOTAL PRICE
70	KOCH	1	37" X 30" steam heated dry tumbler with coils	—		990.00
71	KOCH	1	30" stainless steel laundry chute extractor	—		3400.00
72	KOCH	1	Grindstone	—		1490.00
73	KOCH	1	Beef Line Membrane removal machine, $\frac{3}{4}$ h.p. motor, stainless steel construction with trays			3320.00
74	8669	1	42" X 12'0" stainless steel top packing table, galvanized frame	—		490.00
75	F-M	1	Bench type scale with stainless steel pan, 200-lb. gross capacity	—		990.00
76	5302	1 set	Tracking, 24 all-steel gear-operated switches, 20 all-steel automatic switches, 720 - 12" hangers, 1760'0" of $\frac{1}{2}$" X $2\frac{1}{2}$" track, fabricated			14,200.00
77	1332	2	Fairbanks Track Scales		1590.00	3180.00
78	5396	3	Brake rail, squeeze type, one on kill floor, one boning room, one shipping room		240.00	720.00
79	5312	100	Trolleys, black frame, for forequarters, stainless steel hooks	—	4.50	450.00
80	8021	30	Stainless steel fresh meat trees, 12 hooks, black trolley		20.00	600.00

81	54	1	Jones Band Saw, with totally enclosed 5 h.p. motor and switch		3490.00
82	KOCH	1	Landing table, 12 gauge stainless steel top, galvanized under frame		447.00
83	78691	1	20'0" long moving top boning table with stainless steel belt and $\frac{3}{4}$" X 18" X 48" Durasan boards, stainless steel transfer chute to Lazy Susan, framework hot dip galvanized		14,200.00
84	KOCH	3	Fat conveyor under table	For	1990.00
85	8291	1	Lazy Susan Table		2240.00
86	KOCH	1	Bone Conveyor, 18" wide, approximately 17'0" long and galvanized slide		3490.00
87	12034	1	Multivac		5500.00
88	2145	1	Pump		3210.00
89	8666	2	Stainless steel tables	310.00	620.00
90	8667	3	Box Packing tables, 2'8" X 8'0" with 16 gauge stainless steel top and galvanized frame	350.00	1050.00
91	F-M	2	Bench Scales with stainless steel pans and adjustable stand on wheels, with stainless steel beam and 200-lb gross capacity	1127.00	2254.00
92	KOCH	1	Condemned paunch table with stainless steel top and galvanized manure box with platform		2248.00

ITEM NO.	CAT. NO.	QUANTITY	DESCRIPTION	WEIGHT/CUBE APPROX.	PRICE EACH	TOTAL PRICE
93	KOCH	1	Inedible offal cooling tank, 5'0" X 10'0" X 3'0"			527.00
94	KOCH	1	12" dia. screw conveyor in flared trough. Includes all drive elements and encapsulated motor			4490.00
95	KOCH	1	16" dia. screw conveyor in flared trough. All heavy duty construction. Includes all drive elements, encapsulated motor and hinged cover with hasp for M.I.D. seal			6912.00
96	KOCH	1	Raw material holding bin approximately 382 cu. ft. capacity. Includes discharge screw with all drive elements and en-capsulated motor. Also includes expanded metal cover with hinged access door. Door to have hasp for M.I.D. seal			$5690.00
97	KOCH	1	16" dia. screw conveyor in flared trough. All heavy duty construction. Includes all drive elements, motor, and hinger cover with hasp for M.I.D. seal. Also includes changing chute to Hogor			
98	KOCH	1	21 knife Duke Hogor. Frame and rotor of all steel welded construction, double row spherical roller bearings, coupling and 100 h.p., 1750 rpm encapsulated motor. Also includes structural steel			3980.00

		Qty	Description			Price
99	KOCH	1	base, vibroisolator and steel support staging			12,400.00
100	KOCH	1	16" screw conveyor in standard "U" trough. Includes connecting hopper to bottom of Hogor and connecting chute to blow tank. Also includes all drive elements and encapsulated motor			3910.00
101	KOCH	1	Blow tank, 6' dia. with 14" flanged feed opening and renewable cone section. Includes pressure gauge, safety valves and support legs, built in accord with the ASME Code for 125 # W.P. and bearing National Board Stamp. For cooker having 201 cu. ft. capcity. Also includes 14" gate valve for charging opening and 6" quick opening valve for discharge line			4910.00
102	KOCH	4	Long radius pipe bends for blow-line to include 1 - 180° bend, 1 - 90° bend, and 2 - 45° bends with flanges made on	For		997.00
103	KOCH	1	#8A transfer valve, 6" pipe size, full area, chain and chain wheel operated. Ports at 180°, 45° and 135°			1127.0
	KOCH	2	Dry rendering cookers, 5' dia X 12' long nominal size. 201 cu. ft. capacity. Built to comply with the ASME Code for 90 psi jacket pressure and 45 psi internal pressure and bearing the appropriate code symbols. Standard agitator shaft speed is 38 rpm. Price includes extension neck, safety valve, sampling cock,			

ITEM NO.	CAT. NO.	QUANTITY	DESCRIPTION	WEIGHT/CUBE APPROX.	PRICE EACH	TOTAL PRICE
			air vent and panel board on which is mounted internal and jacket pressure gauges and thermometer. Blow line connection will be installed.			
104	KOCH	1	#5 Drive has 30 h.p. encapsulated motor coupled to herringbone gear reducer driving agitator shaft thry roller chain running in oil in cast housing	—	16,500.00	33,000.00
105	KOCH	1	#5-S Dump Percolator System consisting of 2 drain baskets, 2 pans, 2 chain hoists, platform and screw conveyor with hopper. Hopper has variable speed drive	—	—	9897.00
106	KOCH	1	#39 size 3 rotary tallow pump including base, coupling, relief valve and 2 h.p. encapsulated motor. 1½" suction end discharge	—	—	940.00
			#104-2 Settling Tank, 2 cells each 5' square X 5' deep with 27" cone bottom 19" above floor, making overall height of 9'0". Complete with 2" steam coils, 18" platform with ladder and handrails, 2 thermometers, 2 - 2" swinging suctions, 2 - 2" draw-off openings in cone and 3" opening in bottom of cone. Grease capacity 16,580# level full	—		2980.00

			Description		Amount
107	KOCH	1	#39B Tallow and sludge pump with base and encapsulated motor. 3″ suction end discharge, 2″ maximum particle size		940.00
109	KOCH	1	9″ screw conveyor to transport cooked produce to pressor. In extra heavy duty trough. Includes all drive elements and encapsulated motor		2190.00
110	KOCH	1	7″ Duke Pressor complete with encapsulated motor, automatic hydraulically actuated choke, tallow screw, sectional flights, herringbone gearing, stainless steel feed chute with magnet		31,900.00
111	KOCH	1	Hydraulic Control console for pressor, including variable volume pump and motor, pressure relieving value, solenoid control valve, gauges, control relays for pressor motor, oil reservoir, ammeter and all push buttons with pilot lights		4210.00
112	KOCH	1	Pressor tallow pump consisting of special pump with feed in screw, including base, coupling and ecapsulated motor		2240.00
113	KOCH	1	9″ screw conveyor. All in heavy duty trough. Includes all drive elements, encapsulated motor and water-tight cover on portion outside of building		3790.00

ITEM NO.	CAT. NO.	QUANTITY	DESCRIPTION	WEIGHT/CUBE APPROX.	PRICE EACH	TOTAL PRICE
			Pressed Crax Storage			
114	KOCH	1	10 × 6 Bucket elevator approximately 35'0" overall height. In water-tight housing with all drive elements and encapsulated motor		—	4980.00
115	KOCH	1	12" screw conveyor with water-tight cover, all drive elements and encapsulated motor. Also includes 1 air operated discharge opening for loading trucks		—	3410.00
116	KOCH	1	14' dia. X 25' high A.O. Smith glass lined silo for storing pressed cracklings. Includes mechanical unloader, access ladder, air vents and support kits. Also includes installation supervision		—	17,950.00
117	KOCH	2	Vapor Consensors with 6" inlet and 4" outlet		—	970.00
118	KOCH	1	Hotwell, all steel construction for up to 6 cookers, 4' wide X 8' long X 7' high with vented hood, gas after-burner and thermostatic control baffles		—	2140.00
			Blood Drying			
119	KOCH	2	Raw blood holding tanks approximately 10,000# capacity. Includes support legs and access ladder		2490.00	4980.00
120	KOCH	2	#39B liquid blood pump with base and			

136

No.	Supplier	Qty	Description		
			encapsulated motor. 3″ suction end discharge, 2″ maximum particle size	1247.00	2494.00
121	KOCH	1	#A-715 blood dryer 5′ dia. X 12′ long nominal size. 201 cu. ft. capacity. Built to comply with the ASME Code for 90 psi jacket pressure and 45 psi internal pressure and bearing the appropriate code symbols. Agitator shaft speed to be 26 to 28 rpm. Price includes extension neck with 3″ blood inlet, safety valve, sampling cock, air vent, and panel board on which internal and jacket pressure gauges and thermometer are mounted		16,950.00
122	KOCH	1	Dried blood receiver with screen for removing bones and bagging spouts. Also includes support legs		2140.00
123	KOCH	1	#25 vapor condensor with 6″ inlet and 4″ outlet		970.00
124	KOCH	1	Outside storage tank. This is to be used railroad tank car, with 60,000 # capacity		1910.00
125	KOCH	1	Outside livestock scale, no lumber included		2610.00
126	KOCH F-M	1	Platform scale, overhead suspension, 5′0″ X 5′0″		3110.00
127	KOCH	1	Fold-up retaining cage		997.00
128	KOCH	1 Set	Galvanized rack for dry storage room		1140.00
129	KOCH	1	Box stapler		495.00

ITEM NO.	CAT. NO.	QUANTITY	DESCRIPTION	WEIGHT/CUBE APPROX.	PRICE EACH	TOTAL PRICE
130	706	1	Platform scale - Bone room			310.00
131	KOCH	1	End chute or viscera table - one for punches and one for viscera, galvanized			987.00
132	KOCH	1	Wizard knife, large type 520			990.00
133	2812	1	B&D Dehorning saw with balancer and combination unit			550.00
134	24918	1	Air compressor, 25 h.p. with starter			5410.00
135	KOCH	1	Hide Chute			547.00
136	KOCH	1	Condemned and bone chute by viscera table			942.00
137	1351	1	I-Beam trolley for brisket saw			32.00
138	706	1	Hide Scale			310.00
139	KOCH	1	Chute for viscera to be saved from kill floor to basement, galvanized			890.00
140	1930	4	Tripe trucks		420.00	1680.00
141	KOCH	1	Head rack			89.00
142	KOCH	1	Gravity Feed Trolley Storage Rail			987.00
143	KOCH	1 Set	Galvanized rack in offal cooler for pan from 56289 truck			1127.00
144	5T-24	1	Fully hydraulic pallet wheel truck with polyethylene wheels			420.00

145	KOCH	1	Hide landing table, stainless steel top, galvanized frame. Table to be 5'0" X 5'0" extra heavy duty		790.00
146	8666	1	Inedible offal boxing table		320.00
147	48332	1	24" X 24" stainless steel sink for boning room		220.00
148	48340	1	Faucet for sink		290.00
149	6757	2	Platform trucks for inedibles	75.00	150.00
150	6756	1	Lift jack		62.00
151	6396	10	Hose racks with clean up units	420.00	4200.00
152	KOCH	1	Box stapling for inedible room		275.00
153	KOCH	1	Electric control panels with all starters, fuse disconnect - Push button station with pilot lights, all pre-wired in NEMA 12 enclosure		7980.00
154	KOCH	1	Stainless steel top preliminary viscera separating table		490.00
155	M-34H	1	Casing cleaning machine		4390.00
156	2730-S	1	Stunner		650.00
157	2737	1	Splitting Saw		950.00
158	2366	1	Model 80-J Balancer		220.00
159	2727	1	Saw sterilizer		135.00
160	KOCH	2	Stainless steel slides	450.00	900.00
161	2476	1	Pluck Table		595.00

ITEM NO.	CAT. NO.	QUANTITY	DESCRIPTION	WEIGHT/CUBE APPROX.	PRICE EACH	TOTAL PRICE
162	KOCH	1	Overhead conveyor with track and drive for kill floor			19,870.00
163	5141	1M	Trolleys with gambrels		4.20	4200.00
164	1932	15	Sterilizing lavatories		145.00	2175.00
163	1932-555	17	Knife boxes		29.00	493.00
166	1930	5	Offal hanging trucks		420.00	2100.00
167	3736	6	Offal pan trucks		300.00	1800.00
168	1332-33	2	Track scales		1620.00	3240.00
169	13475	6	Casing trucks		190.00	1140.00
170	KOCH	—	Overhead track system			4987.00
171	7987-1	1	Hoist			590.00
172	1236	1	Hog restrainer			2990.00
173	5597	1	Hog Hoist			3400.00
174	KOCH	1 Set	Bleeding Rail			997.00
174	5522 Spec	1	Hog scalding vat with chute and platform			4990.00
176	5576	1	Dehairer with 10 h.p. motor			6810.00
177	5583	1	Gambreling table			920.00
178	KOCH	1	Automatic singeing unit			3420.00
179	KOCH	1	3-level shroud platform			1200.00
180	KOCH	1	Automatic shower			990.00

No.	Cat. No.	Qty	Description		Amount
181	5601 Spec	1	Moving top viscera inspection table with platform		19,400.00
182	66509	1	Viscera separating table		720.00
183	7101	1	Head table		600.00
184	2040	1	Board for Table		50.00
185	2440	1	Blood drain		65.00
186	7215	1	Fat wash box		490.00
187	87024	1	Leaf lard platform		320.00
188	KOCH	1	Roller sticking conveyor		3990.00
189	KOCH	1	Hog hair chute		621.00
190	KOCH	2	250 h.p. boiler with condensate return system and hot water storage tank		49,870.00
191	KOCH	—	To furnish the refrigeration system. Two compressors for beef chill, two compressors for beef holding, two compressors for hog chill, one compressor for offal, one compressor for boning and one compressor for freezer; also the necessary coil for the coolers		198,000.00
192	4598A G.S.	1	5'0" X 11'2" track cooler door with vestibule door also		3210.00
193	4598A G.G.	5	5'0" X 11'2" track cooler door	1200.00	600.00
194	14569	1	Track vestibule door, 5'0" X 11'2"		820.00
195	14560	1	Cooler door, 5'0" X 6'6"		590.00

ITEM NO.	CAT. NO.	QUANTITY	DESCRIPTION	WEIGHT/CUBE APPROX.	PRICE EACH	TOTAL PRICE
196	47003	3	Dock Seals		400.00	1200.00
197	14548	1	Freezer door, 5'0" X 6'6"			820.00
198	6907 6715	1	Hand operated jack and pallet for frozen product transportation			240.00
199	5041	10	Boning hooks		2.00	20.00
200	7909	3M	Shroud pins		For	220.00
201	50013	50#	Deadlocks		For	25.00
202	1132	6 gal.	Ink		For	40.00
203	1990	2	Ink marking brushes		7.50	15.00
204	7952	500	Shrouds		For	731.00
205	6145	48	Skinning knives		3.70	177.60
206	5194	24	Sticking knives		For	50.00
207	6320	30	Steels		5.40	192.00
208	6336	30	Scabbards		4.90	147.00
209	7947	1	Shroud roller			56.00
210	1320	2	Wellsaws		135.00	270.00
211	KOCH	1	Cervin Electric livestock driving prod			590.00
212	578	2	Roller poles		19.00	38.00
213	752	2	Shovels		27.00	54.00
214	1555	2	Offal Branders		75.00	150.00

Item	Code	Qty	Description	Unit	Total
215	1570	1	U.S. Stamp Marker		8.50
216	1547	1	U.S. Stamp Marker, long handle		16.00
217	1589	5M	Stes hide and carcass ind. tags		69.00
218	1590	2500 gangs	Tags with numbers		200.00
219	84	12	Frocks		89.00
220	59009	24	Boots	6/80.00	320.00
221	58731	10	Metal Mesh Gloves	22.00	220.00
222	1642	15	Safety caps	4.00	60.00
223	336	4	Floor Squeegee		29.00
224	KOCH	1	Wash-up pump with detergent tank		790.00
225	5075	200	Car Hooks	.56	112.00
226	KOCH	1	Stainless steel shroud pin box		40.00
227	504	10M	Skewers		27.00
228	510	1M	Neck pins		16.50
229	7915	1M	Beef bags - hinds		17.00
230	7926	1M	Beef bags - fores		15.00
231	KOCH	1	Weasand rod		47.00
232	3633	4	Inedible drum with labels		140.00
233	1010	4	Trash cans		140.00
234	1005	24	Liners		65.00
235	7221	1	Inspector's Desk		140.00

ITEM NO.	CAT. NO.	QUANTITY	DESCRIPTION	WEIGHT/CUBE APPROX.	PRICE EACH	TOTAL PRICE
236	1761	1	Knife Sharpener			170.00
237	77025	6	25'-0" Hose Section		39.00	234.00
238	40772	6	Nozzles		9.00	54.00
239	1421	3	Dial thermometers for water line		54.00	162.00
240	6554	24	Aprons		4.20	100.80
241	1655	4	Stainless steel meat drums		110.00	440.00
242	6060	48	Boning knives		3.90	187.20
243	6078	12	Breaking knives		7.50	90.00
244	2678	24	3-locker sections		99.00	2376.00
245	1825	1	Cash knocker, extra			220.00
246	1922	2	Bone trucks		320.00	640.00
247	6705	4	Boxed meat pallet trucks		220.00	880.00
248	6715	2	Lift jacks		75.00	150.00
249	5282	200	On-the-rail trolleys - extra		4.95	990.00
250	1554	1	Offal brander - extra			85.00
251	1570	1	U.S. stamp - extra			8.50
252	1547	1	U.S. stamp hammer type - extra			16.00
253	755	12	Metal sponges			5.90
254	754	2	Stainless steel shovels		21.00	42.00

255	7409	3	Beef shifter	89.00	267.00
256	1507	3	Meat trucks	350.00	1050.00
257	KOCH	6	Overhead spray valves	35.00	210.00
258	KOCH	1	Air line dryer and valves		495.00
259	KOCH	15	Galvanized pans for 56289 truck	39.00	585.00
260	9101	55 gal.	Oil for trolleys		97.00
261	9103	100#	Spec. TAK-1000 trolley cleaning compound		85.00
262	KOCH	20	Hardwood pallets	7.00	140.00
263	KOCH	1	Oil pump for equipment-oiling of equipment		195.00
264	1097	2	Electric saw cords	17.00	34.00
			TOTAL - QUOTED EQUIPMENT F.O.B. FACTORY		$829,457.00

APPENDIX C
LIST OF EMPLOYEE POSITIONS

LIST OF EMPLOYEES

Function	Number	Function	Number
Unskilled			
Drive in Kill	1	First Transfer	2
Stun	2	Clean Rump	2
Shackle	2	Second Transfer	2
Sticker (Bleeder)	5	Rim Over	1
Drop-Scald-Dehair	3	High Siding	2
Gambrel	2	Low Siding	2
Singeing and Shaving	6	Pull Hide	2
Eviscerate	3	Sever Briskets	1
Split	1	Saw	2
Scale	3	Trim	2
Push to Cooler	3	Wash	1
Push Carcasses in Cooler	1	Push Trucks	2
Packers	4	Yard Men	2
Driver	1	Clean-Up Men	3
Scalping	2	Shroud	2
Sever Heads	1	Additional Employees	12
Flush Heads	4		
Skilled			
Trim Lard	3	Work Offal	2
Break Carcasses	4	Work Heads	2
Boners	6	Mechanics	3
Shipping Clerks	2	Truck Driver	1
Rendering Operators	2	Additional Employees	2
Work Edibles & Inedibles	2		

Marketing Research Associates

FEASIBILITY STUDY

TRAVEL TRAILER PARK

Anytown, U.S.A.

Prepared by

Robert E. Stevens, Ph.D.
Philip K. Sherwood, Ed.D.

STEVENS-SHERWOOD AND ASSOCIATES
2140 S. 78th E. Ave.
Tulsa, Oklahoma

CERTIFICATION

We hereby certify that we have no interest, present or contemplated, in the proposed Travel Trailer Park and that to the best of our knowledge and belief, the statements and information contained in this report are correct—subject to the limitations herein set forth.

_____

Robert E. Stevens, Ph.D.

_____

Philip K. Sherwood, Ed.D.

TABLE OF CONTENTS

LIST OF TABLES

INTRODUCTION

The purpose of this study is two-fold:

1. To develop the background, criteria and process of selecting a suitable location for a medium size travel trailer park in the Northwest Canton region and

2. To set forth basic facts, economic projections, demand analysis, competition analysis, social considerations, governmental factors, conclusions and recommendations relative to the development of a travel trailer or recreational vehicle park.

The study focuses on the economic feasibility of investing and managing a travel trailer park facility with a maximum initial development cost in the range of $200,000 to $250,000.

The specific objectives of the study are to:

1. Evaluate past national and regional trends in the recreational vehicle and outdoor recreation industries.

2. Determine and analyze those factors which have characterized the growth and development of travel trailer parks.

3. Determine present and potential market and demand patterns.

4. Evaluate competition.

5. Formulate plans, objectives, and goals for developing, marketing, and managing a travel trailer park.

6. Make financial projections.

7. Evaluate the returns of the proposed investment.

SCOPE AND LIMITATIONS

It should be pointed out that two factors beyond the scope of this study could significantly affect the outcome of an RV park. One of these is the energy problems faced by the United States and the possible problems this would entail in terms of availability of gasoline and price of gasoline. No attempt has been made to forecast these events. Another factor influencing the success of the proposed park is the possible recession and/or deflation anticipated by many economists. No attempt has been made to forecast these events.

It should also be pointed out that no attempt was made to analyze the managerial abilities of administrative personnel of the proposed operation. This was beyond the scope of the project. However, the profitability of any business is dependent on the possession of adequate managerial skills by those personnel responsible for the decision making within the organization.

The study highlights conclusions and recommendations, an overview of the tourism and recreation market in general and in Northwest Canton, then proceeds to a competitive analysis of existing private facilities and the resulting most viable marketing strategy. The study concludes with a site and location analysis, a financial feasibility analysis, and an analysis of an existing park for sale.

CONCLUSIONS AND RECOMMENDATIONS

Based on the results of the analysis undertaken in this study, the following conclusions have been drawn:

*Locate near population center—this will be future trend. Also, has the advantage if gasoline prices cause campers to make shorter trips in the future.

*Locate on south or west shorelines of Cat Lake, near a dominant recreation attraction or close to an existing high amenity destination-type park.

*Consider investment in a combination travel trailer (RV) and mobile home (MH) park, but locate to maximize the recreation vehicle aspect of the development.

*A park having many amenities has lowest risk, and the trend is definitely toward "destination type" parks. Of course, this type of park requires higher investment.

*The quality of park's development and the extent of its improvements depends on local demand, the amount of rent you can collect, and what amenities the competition is offering. Analysis of the market suggests that the greatest need relative to competition is to:

1. Develop a new park (or purchase and improve an existing park) which offers amenities at the high end of the range (similar to Safari located on Highway 10).

2. Price rental space just below the market at $7.00 per unit (includes all amenities except extra people).

3. Offer the following amenities: fishing, boating, grocery store, laundry, restrooms, vending machines, group shelter, picnic area, playground, children facilities, recreation building, and all hookups.

4. Park size should be in the range of 40 spaces to 100 spaces.

*Marketing strategy should include:

1. Price slightly below the high amenity parks.

2. Heavy promotional activities, especially on signs from major highways.

3. Strong consumer orientation to encourage repeat business.

*Management strategy should include:

1. A professional approach to managing the business through setting income and occupancy goals; developing sound policies for resident behavior in and about the premises; dealing effectively with the local community.

2. An aggressive approach to improving occupancy levels by appropriate marketing.

3. Effective cost control system to minimize expenses and sound inventory management (store goods).

4. Effective skills to handle resident complaints and trouble-makers—particularly the noise problem.

TOURISM AND RECREATION—AN INDUSTRY OVERVIEW

The concept of a travel trailer park brings consideration of the tourism and recreation industries of which it is a part. This section of the report highlights current trends in tourism and recreation at both a national-state level and specifically in Northwest Canton.

One basic question which must be dealt with in light of both energy and inflation is the future of both tourism and recreation. Tourism expenditures are influenced by both inflation and energy problems, and recreational expenditures are mainly influenced by inflation. All available evidence suggests that the problems that beset these industries in the early 1970's have not led to the sluggishness that was predicted. The availability of gasoline at relatively stable prices and increases in personal income have both worked to offset a decline in these industries.

There are also indications that a growing proportion of families consider travel and vacation a necessity rather than a luxury. Responses to energy shortages and inflation are more likely to be shorter, less expensive trips than a cancellation of planned activities.

Another strong indication of the current strength is the strong showing of recreational vehicles in terms of total shipments following the "energy scare." Most of the increase has been in motor homes and travel trailers which accounted for about 60% of total recreational vehicle shipments in 1980. Complete statistics on shipment are shown in Appendix A.

These facts lead to an assumption of continued growth in travel and recreational activities generally and specifically in Northwest Canton.

TOURISM AND RECREATION—NORTHWEST CANTON

The state of Canton in general and Northwest Canton in particular have developed and supported a great deal of tourist and recreational-oriented attractions in the last decade. The development of the Cat Dam and Reservoir gave impetus to more rapid development of the area.

Northwest Canton has moved from the second ranking area for overnight visitors in 1974 to the first rank in 1976, 1978, and 1980. Of the total 24,107,500 overnight visitors to Canton in 1980, about 22% were in Northwest Canton (see Table 1).

TABLE I

Overnight Visitors Northwest Canton: 1980

County	Visitors	State Share
Benson	2,543,340	10.55%
Carrollton	2,143,155	8.89%
Madisonville	26,515	.11%
Webster	605,100	2.51%
TOTALS	5,318,110	22.06%

Sources: Tourism in Canton, 1980

Thus Benson County attracts the greatest number of overnight visitors. Although Webster County is far behind as an attractor, it leads the entire Northwest Canton region as the economic and population center. As such, Webster County can be a source of weekend business during the slow seasons.

Overnight Campers

Of specific interest in the feasibility of the travel trailer facility is the number of overnight campers. As is shown in the Table 2 for the state, overnight campers accounted for about 6.6% of the overnight visitors in 1980.

TABLE 2
CAMPING ACTIVITY IN CANTON
For the Years 1976–1980

	1976	1978	1980
Overnight Campers	$ 1,626,100	$ 1,714,064	$ 1,573,511
Parties	460,028	451,069	403,464
Avg. Stay (nights)	7.4	6.8	7.6
Persons per party	3.6	3.8	3.9
Person-night	12,255,140	11,655,635	11,958,684
Spent per party-night	$31.45	$33.87	$35.97
Annual Economic Impact	$107,062.316	$103,888,401	$110,295,762
Percent by Category			
Truck-camp	33.5%	32.0%	32.5%
RV-camp	49.6%	50.0%	49.0%
Tent-camp	16.9%	18.0%	18.5%
TOTAL	100.0%	100.0%	100.0%
Trip-nights	3,404,107	3,067,269	3,066,326

Source: Tourism in Canton, 1980 edition, page 6.
Note: Camping statistics are based on State Park Superintendent monthly reports, private campground owner surveys, U.S. Corps of Engineers and National Forest Service monthly reports. Camper expenditures are based on estimates of the National 3M Company.

More pertinent to this study is the number of group-nights as shown in Table 3. That is the total number of parties (3 to 4 people) times the number of nights stay in a particular area. These calculations are shown following for the state in total and then estimated for Northwest Canton.

TABLE 4

Northwest Canton Population and Income Statistics

County	Population				Medium Effective Buying Income per Household			
	1960[1]	1970[1]	1975[1]	1978[2]	1960[2]	1970[2]	1975[2]	1978[2]
Benson	36,372	50,476	59,700	61,200	$4,086	$7,257	$8,660	$12,133
Carrollton	11,284	12,301	14,000	14,800	3,708	5,935	6,478	8,854
Madisonville	9,068	9,453	10,100	10,800	3,851	5,249	5,681	8,052
Webster	55,797	77,370	89,400	93,100	4,688	9,134	9,624	13,056

Sources: 1. State and County Economic Data for Canton, Industrial Research and Extension Center, University of Canton

2. Survey of Buying Power, Sales Management Magazine, June-Aug. 1968, 1971, 1976, 1978

160

has been established, and there is a very favorable political and resident attitude toward progress.

COMPETITIVE ANALYSIS

There are three basic marketing strategies used by private trailer park facilities. One strategy is aimed at the "overnight" or "pass thru" market. This park is designed to appeal to travelers enroute to some predetermined destination or those who are in a location for a short (one to three-day) period. These parks are usually close to major highways and offer a few amenities to guests.

A second strategy is aimed at those travelers who are planning an extended stay (four to seven days) in a particular area—usually a resort area or other major tourist attraction. While the trailer park does not contain many amenities, it is located very close to, if not adjacent to the amenities. This would be the situation where a park is located next to a Corps of Engineers recreation area on a lake.

A third strategy is still aimed at the extended traveler, but the park itself offers all or most of the amenities and may or may not be located close to other amenities. The park thus becomes the attraction in and of itself and offers facilities and services geared to guests who will remain in the area for a few days.

All three of these strategies are being used in the region of Canton under consideration. The major competitors in the Webster-Benson County area are shown in Table 5.

Table 5 showing facilities offered by different competitors clearly demonstrates the differences in services offered in this area. Jellystone park is by far the most complete—using the concept of a resort in itself; it

TABLE 3

CAMPER PARTY NIGHTS: STATE AND REGION

	STATE			NORTHWEST REGION*		
	1976	1978	1980	1976	1978	1980
Parties	460,028	451,069	403,464	93,754	99,100	89,004
Average Stay	7.4	6.8	7.6	7.4	6.8	7.6
Party Nights	3,404,207	3,067,269	3,066,326	693,378	673,880	676,430

*These figures are conservative for Northwest Canton since the use of camping facilities would not be proportionate to total visitors in an area. Northwest Canton has a higher than proportionate demand for this type of facility.

These two tables (Tables 3 and 4) together show that in 1980, for example, 89,004 camping parties came to Northwest Canton, stayed an average of 7.6 days, and demanded 334,833 R-V campsites and 120,404 tent campsites. The two explicit assumptions in these calculations are that Northwest Canton's share of campers is at least equal to its share of all overnight visitors, and that the percentages of campers by type is the same in Northwest Canton as for the state as a whole.

Data supplied by the Corps of Engineers, shown in Appendix B, reveals that Cat Lake is one of the most popular resort areas in the state by visitation counts and has also experienced rapid growth in the last nine years. Specific data on Cat Lake shows that Hickory Creek and Bill's Creek are the two most popular park areas on Cat Lake. Both have experienced increased usage in the last five years.

Northwest Canton Economic Development

An important factor in the feasibility of any business is the health of the environment in which the firm must operate. This section presents data on per capita income and population for the area.

Table 4 shows a substantial growth in population and per capita income in the four-county area—especially in Benson and Webster Counties. In these two counties, a 6% increase in population and almost a 300% increase in average household effective buying income occurred between 1966 and 1978 estimates. Population projections for Benson-Webster Counties are 163,073 for 1980 and 179,158 for 1985. This would reflect a 16% increase in population for the two-county area between 1978 estimates and 1985. Clearly, this is one of the major growth areas in Canton during the next decade.

Thus, a good base for future development and expansion of the area

TABLE 5
RV TRAILER PARKS
BY TYPE OF AMENITIES

RV Trailer Park	Coffee Snack Bar	Group Shelter	Restrooms	Laundry room	Swimming pool	Sanitary Dump	Showers	Picnic Tables	Rec Room	Boats	Teen Hut	Planned activities	All Hookups	Tennis Courts	Barbeque Grill	Tent Area	Playground	Number of Units
KOA (Highway 12)	X		X	X	X	X	X	X	X				X			X	X	60
Jellystone Park (Highway 80)	X	X	X	X	X	X	X	X	X	X	X	X	X	X	X	X	X	60
Sofari (Highway 10) (Country 30)	X		X	X	X	X	X			X						X	X	24*
Jim John's Trailer Park (Hickory Creek Rec. Area)					X							X						39
Carrol's Mobile Home Park (Highway 78, Lucedale)					X				X									10**

*Currently Expanding—will double capacity

** Approximate

offers the full range of services. KOA and Sofari are basically using the same strategy but with fewer amenities. KOA's location on Highway 12 also appeals to overnighters. Sofari unit is being expanded at the present time.

The Jim John's Trailer Park is using the strategy of not providing amenities but locating close to them. It is within 200 yards of the Corps of Engineers Hickory Creek Recreational Area. It offers nothing more than a place to park your trailer, but a store, boats, bait, picnic tables, and so on are all within 500 yards of the park.

A couple of mobile home parks offer overnight hookups but are catering strictly to overnighters and probably the "overflow" of other RV parks.

A new proposed park located only 100 yards off the Highway 78 north of Lucedale is planned and is waiting a zoning decision. Judging from the location and amount of land used in development, it would appear to be aimed at the "pass thru" or short stay market.

The RV park industry offers special opportunities today for investment in destination type parks.

The overnight RV park is, in general, a poor investment. The reason is that major oil companies will take over this business in coming years. Their concept makes private investment in overnight spaces impractical. The authors have learned the oil companies have a long-term plan to open overnight stops in conjunction with service stations. Facilities will be spartan and rates very low. Each station will have only minimum spaces (10–50), and the goal is more service station business. Service station personnel will operate the parks . . . so, there is little or no management expense. Many such parks are already in operation.

The real opportunities in the RV park business are destination parks. These parks, in the main, are close to major population centers (two to four hours driving time or less) and offer urban RV owners a chance for fun on weekends and during vacations away from home. Such parks require a major financial commitment because they require many activities to keep guests busy. Typical of such facilities are: swimming, fishing, boating, golf (including miniature golf); children's playgrounds; horses; snowmobiles; skiing; separate recreational building for adults, teenagers, and children; tennis; hayrides; picnic areas; ping pong; shuffleboard; horseshoes; archery; hiking and bicycle trails; restaurant/bars; general store; laundries; movies; and so on. Most important is a planned recreation program for children, teenagers, and adults. Such parks earn about half of their revenue from fees other than for space. The goal is fun . . . fun . . . fun for everybody so the visitor stays longer and returns often.

A second category of destination parks requires less investment in facilities but usually land cost is high. Located near major attractions, such as a Disneyland, visitors are attracted by fun and sightseeing activities outside the park.

RV park rates are rising fast. But not so fast that RV travel isn't a big saving over other modes of travel. The increase comes due to rising costs, of course, but even more because RV buyers are affluent and will pay more to get more in the way of deluxe park facilities.

We would caution the RV park developer to ignore the overnight park, although the destination park does accept overnight visitors. Although the risk of return for a successful RV investment is higher than for the MH park, the risk is much higher. Feasibility studies for RV parks are much more subject to error; in contrast, such studies for mobile home parks are almost fool-proof. One problem with RV park investments is that mortgage money is more difficult to obtain than for the mobile home park. The financial community knows of the long successful record for MH parks. The RV park is much newer and has no well-established financial record.

DEVELOPING A VIABLE MARKETING STRATEGY

One consistent observation of private non-franchised trailer parks is the lack of an effective marketing program. This section of the report will outline major considerations of the marketing activities which would be a part of the overall management of any park.

Target Market

Every attempt should be made to identify potential customers of the services offered by the RV park. This market, like all others, is composed of several segments:

1. Cross-country travelers enroute to a predetermined destination looking strictly for overnight hookups.

2. Cross-country travelers enroute to a specific area of the country but with no definite destination in mind—looking for some overnight and some short stay (two to four days) accommodations.

3. Local area residents—usually weekenders on short trips with a predetermined destination—tourist attraction, horse show, lake recreation area, etc. in mind. Mostly want overnight hookups but also need some short stay accommodations.

4. RV clubs, large multi-unit family groups, sport spectators, etc. These may be local area residents and/or non-local residents, depending on the nature of the group involved. They may want only overnight accommodations for a short stay.

The marketing mix—location, amenities, price, promotion, etc.— developed should be put together with specific groups in mind. For example, a strictly overnight park would be located close to a major highway, offer few amenities, and not require a park there. The following diagram shows some of the possible positions available for a new park attempting to "fit in" with existing offerings.

Low Amenities				High Amenities
Bill's Mobile Home Park	Jim John's Travel Trailer Park	KOA	Sofari	Yogi Bear's Park

The current trend in travel trailer parks is in the direction of the high amenity Yogi Bear Park concept. Appealing to the extended stay (five to seven days) market with a complete array of amenities from laundry rooms to planned activities for children. At the other end of the scale is the mobile home park that has a few sites for travel trailers and offers no specific amenities for the traveler.

Placement somewhere close to the Sofari-Yogi Bear end of the spectrum with the amenities appears to be the best fit given the nature of demand and competition. Especially if a location close to a major highway is selected, a broader appeal can be developed to attract the overnight or short stay groups.

Product Place

Offer a fairly accessible location, close to big attractions and metro-politan areas with a fully developed park theme. Park theme includes name of park, architecture style, landscaping and promotion. Requires more creative thinking than anything else (including money). For example, if a western theme were chosen, then the name of the park should be western in nature, landscaping should be western in nature, streets or driveways given western names, store should be western in appearance, and so on. This gives the whole park a personality and excitement found in the more progressive parks.

Probably 40 to 100 sites either constructed or at least available for development will be most feasible. All hookups should be provided with other amenities such as a swimming pool, laundry, bath area, store, covered shelter, picnic tables, a must.

Price

The price charged should reflect three things: competition, amenities offered, and usage or costs associated with serving a guest.

More amenities mean a higher price—people understand and accept this. A current price structure reflecting these factors would be as follows:

All hookups (2 people)	$7.50
Water and electricity	7.00
No hookups	5.50
Charge for each additional person	.50
Air conditioner or heater	1.00

This price structure reflects current competitive price for a park with several amenities but also charges those that use a service more than non-users. Basic level of prices reflects number of amenities offered. John's Trailer Park currently offers no amenities and charges a flat rate of $4.00 a night.

Promotion

Travelers, unless they have been with you before, don't know where you are located, what you offer, or how to get to your location. Promotional activities must accomplish this for you. Highway signs with additional arrow signs to your location are a must. Also, listings in national travel guides should be acquired since these are used extensively by travelers.

Any time that a list of names of a travel trailer club or group can be located by direct mail advertising or by a telephone call, it can bring in business. Aggressive selling and promotion will produce good results since few operators appear to be doing anything about seeking out and seling to new customers. Every customer who stays with you is a potential for another stay—get his name and address and you will also have a source of names and word-of-mouth advertising for your operation. Good service will bring more new customers and bring back old customers. Poor service, obviously, has the reverse effects.

SITE AND LOCATION ANALYSIS

A thorough analysis of Northwest Canton suggests that the Cat Lake area represents the best choice for a new recreation vehicle park development.* Several important reasons support the Cat Lake area in general and the south and/or west shorelines in particular:

*Cat Lake is the dominant attraction in Northwest Canton which generates demand for groups of campers and for campers who stay four or more days.

*Within one hour's driving time there are several tourist attractions including:

—Ichaban Sports/Recreation Center and Oriental Restaurant on Highway 27 between Lucedale and Stevensville.

—Hunt's Springs on Highway 60 about 30 miles northeast of Stevensville (on the eastern part of Cat Lake). This resort area is the location of an outdoor theater production which has a national reputation.

—Big Eagle, Hickory Creek, and Bill's Creek (located on the south and west shorelines) are the most popular points for visitors according to the Corps of Engineers.

—Huntsville, which is the home of the University of Canton, and the area's population, employment, economic, educational, and cultural center.

*Accessibility from both U.S. Highway 60 and U.S. Highway 78, the major thoroughfare from Bluff City to points south.

The impact of all these features is that proposed park site will have higher occupancy because camper groups will stay in the area longer. In addition, the combined drawing power of several attractions will enhance

---

*Data supplied by Webster District of the Corps of Engineers 1972–80.

170

repeat business year after year. Such considerations are important for the economic feasibility of destination-type travel trailer parks.

A survey was undertaken for an area south and west of Cat Lake, as discussed above. It established the following:

1. There is a need for additional recreational vehicle or travel trailer spaces in the area. Past growth plus current plans for constructing a new park support this conclusion. For example, the Sofari campground is currently expanding to double its capacity. Also investors are seeking rezoning of the land on Highway 78 between Lucedale and Stevensville for a RV Park development.

2. The park should contain some tent sites and no more than 100 travel trailer spaces. This is based on past and projected growth in demand.

3. The market is likely to grow at the rate of 4% to 8% per year, therefore, future expansion is a possibility.

4. Rentals should be $7.00 per space per night (includes all charges except extra occupancy—i.e., over two persons).

5. Depending on the quality of management, the park should achieve between 20% and 33% occupancy level for the first year's operation. (This is based on 360 days per year.) Based on a seven-month season the park should achieve between 35% and 55% occupancy level during the first year. Aggressive marketing and management of the park should achieve the 55% occupancy level or higher.

The following criteria should be used in selecting a park site:

1. Locate close to a dominant recreation attraction or close to an existing destination-type park. Locations on the highway are more expensive, are oriented to the overnight market, and are more risky ventures due to more intensive future competition. It would be desirable to obtain advertising/sign space on the major highway.

2. Utilities should be close at hand.

3. Terrain should be relatively flat but slightly sloping to provide water runoff. Watch out for slopes and topography which will require extensive grading.

4. Local building codes and zoning should allow a density of spaces per acre to permit profitable operation (up to ten units per acre).

5. Accessibility should include a paved road to the park site.

An analysis of facilities offered by the competition has led to the following specifications:

1. A minimum of 10 acres, preferably 10 acres or more.

2. A minimum of 40 spaces; a maximum of 100 spaces.

3. A combination registration office and grocery store (living quarters added to the rear of the store).

4. Recreation Room, a minimum of 400 square feet.

5. A laundry/restroom facility of about 625 square feet for every 30 to 35 spaces.

6. A small swimming pool—20' X 40'.

7. Crushed rock streets.

8. A public pay telephone.

9. Picnic tables and grills.

10. Covered group shelter and picnic area.

11. Playground.

FINANCIAL FEASIBILITY

Analysis of the macro and micro demand and competition elements substantiate the market feasibility of a recreational vehicle park in the Cat Lake area (south or west side of the lake).

Attention is now directed to the financial feasibility of a park. The presentation will begin with the initial financial status and capital investment schedule. The first year estimated income statements will be developed for four different size parks: 40, 50, 60, and 100 sites. The pro forma income and expense statements for three years will be developed. Finally, investment returns and risks will be evaluated.

Certain assumptions have been stated at the outset of the study:

1. Total investment should not exceed $200,000 to $250,000.

2. Funds for equity investment limited to $50,000.

3. Interest on mortgage or SBA loan is 11.0%.

4. Loan term is 20 years.

5. Land prices of $3,000 per acre.

DEVELOPMENT COSTS

In figuring costs of land and improvements, the developer must recognize the following factors which will influence the amount of investment:

*The source of water supply

*Method of waste treatment

*The amount of work the owner will perform

*Topography—its influence on grading, etc.

Taking the above into consideration, the following Table 6 shows development costs for four (4) different sizes of parks: 40, 50, 60, and 100 sites. All four of these park sizes fall within the market feasibility as analyzed in the area survey on demand and competition trends.

These costs estimates are considered reasonable but approximate. Accurate costs cannot be identified until contractors see the specific site.

TABLE 6

ITEM	40 SITE PARK	50 SITE PARK	60 SITE PARK	100 SITE PARK	DEPR. RATE
Land (1)	$ 45,000	$ 45,000	$ 45,000	$ 45,000	0%
Basic Bldg & Recreation Room (2)	50,000	50,000	50,000	50,000	5%
Restroom & Laundry (3)	8,000	12,000	12,000	16,000	5%
Tables, Grills, & Playgrounds	4,500	5,500	6,500	11,000	10%
Swimming and Wading Pools	14,000	14,000	14,000	14,000	10%
Electricity to sites (4)	6,000	7,000	8,000	12,000	5%
Water to sites (5)	5,200	6,000	6,800	10,000	5%
Sewage hook-ups & collection lines (6)	6,000	7,000	8,000	12,000	5%
Roads and grading (7)	10,000	11,000	12,000	16,000	5%
Supervision and Misc.	15,000	15,000	15,000	15,000	
Total Costs	$163,700	$172,500	$177,300	$201,000	

Notes:

1) Land of 15 acres @ $2,500 per acre

2) Basic building includes registration, store and living quarters—2100 square feet recreation room 400 square feet; total of 2,500 square feet @ $20.00 per square foot.

3) Laundry: 10' by 25', two (2) washers, two (2) dryers, vending machines. Assume all machines are owned by others.

Restrooms Men's: Three (3) showers, two (2) toilets, two (2) urinals, three (3) wash basins, 15' X 12.5'.

Restroom Women's: Three (3) showers, four (4) toilets, three (3) wash basins, 15' X 12.5'.
Total Laundry and Restrooms = 625 square feet.

4) $2,000 fixed charge plus $100.00 per space

5) $2,000 fixed charge plus $80.00 per space

6) $2,000 fixed charge plus $100.00 per space

7) $6,000 fixed charge plus $100.00 per space

From the estimated development costs and other data collected, the proposed project's financial feasibility is now evaluated. First, an analysis of the projected first year's income and expenses will help identify the most appropriate park size: 40, 50, 60, and 100 spaces. Then a five-year pro forma income projection will be made.

Notes to Table 7, Proposed Recreational Vehicle Park, Projected Income Statement by Park Size and Occupancy Level, follow:

1. Assume a seven (7) month season (200 days).

    a. occupancy level one = 35% on base of 210 days or 20% on 360 days

    b. occupancy level two = 45% on base of 210 days or 26% on 360 days.

    c. occupancy level three = 55% on base of 210 days or 32% on 360 days.

    Space Rents = $7.00 per night.

2. Extra Occupancy. Assume 5% of space income (this is low since average party size is 2.9 persons).

3. $.25/space/night.

4. $.25/space/night/net (no investment).

5. $5.00/space night.

175

6. Total income does not include possible tent site rentals.

7. CGS = 60%; 40% markup on retail.

8. Salaries = $1,500 per month 2 men @ $750/mo. for 7 months.

9. Payroll Taxes = 15% of payroll.

10. Property Taxes = 1.5% of $200,000 property value.

11. Insurance = 1.5% of building.

12. Telephone = $50.00/mo. for business and listing.

13. Electricity $1,000 + $.50/camper night.

14. Water = $700 + $.20/camper night.

15. Depreciation straight line based on depreciation rates in Table.

The above assumptions are based on analysis of income statements from the following sources:

1. Institute of Business Planning, REAL ESTATE INVESTMENT PLANNING. Vol. 1.

2. David Nulsen and Robert Nulsen, HANDBOOK FOR DEVELOPING AND OPERATING MOBILE HOME AND RECREATIONAL VEHICLE PARKS. Beverly Hills, CA Trail-R-Club of America.

The bottom line on Table 7 shows net income before income taxes and debt service (mortgage payment). Note that depreciation, a non-cash expense, is included as an expense. It is clear, based on the stated assumptions that either a 60-space or a 100-space park is most feasible from a financial point of view. Of course, under each of the alternative sizes, the higher the occupancy level, the more profitable the operation.

For emphasis, it is important to restate the major assumption in the above financial feasibility analysis: A conservative 7-month or 210-day season is used with occupancy levels of 35%, 45%, and 55%. These levels translate into annual (360-day base) occupancy levels of 20%, 26%, and 32% respectively. The length of the season and the assumed occupancy levels are judged to be quite conservative in relation to the existing and expected future market potential.

Following is a five-year pro forma income projection based on a 60-space recreational vehicle park. The bottom line of Table 8 shows net operating profit (after deduction for depreciation but before income taxes and debt service) rising from $16,500 in 1979 to nearly $39,000 in 1983—an increase of 135% over the five-year period. These projections are based on aggressive management and marketing practices and a willingness of management to be competitive in offering a total amenity package. Occupancy levels will increase through repeat business only if campers have a number of alternative activities to meet their recreational needs.

The investment analysis shows that a total investment of $183,000 will require $55,000 in equity since it will be difficult to secure a mortgage loan in principal amount for more than 70% loan to value ratio ($128,000).

The return on investment calculations show a first year return of 14.7 percent* (See Table 9). This is not spectacular but definitely acceptable for the first year's operation. Aggressive management will be required: (1) increasing rental rates, six percent a year, (2) increasing occupancy levels two to three percentage points per year, and (3) holding expenses down to six percent per year. Under the above conditions the return on investment increases to a desirable 34.7** (see Table 9).

During the first full year of operation, the sum of salaries and net cash flow is in excess of $20,000. This amount does not include "free" rent on living quarters. By the time the fifth year has been completed, the sum of payroll and net cash flow has risen to a healthy $38,552. Taking into consideration a 6 percent per year rate of inflation, the $38,552 is equal to $28,770 in today's purchasing power.

---

*Net Cash Flow in first year of $8,087 divided by equity of $55,000.

**Net Cash Flow in fifth year of $23,302 divided by equity of $67,400 (see Table 9).

TABLE 7
Proposed Recreational Vehicle Park
Projected Income Statement
By Park Size and Occupancy Level

	1	2	3
	FORTY (40) SITE PARK		
Based on 7 month season (210 days)	OCCUPANCY LEVEL		
	35%	45%	55%
Gross Income	2940	3780	4620
Space Rents (1)	20580	26468	32340
Extra Occupancy (2)	1029	1323	1617
Vending Machines (3) Laundry (4)	1470	1890	2310
Store Sales (5)	14700	18900	23100
Total Income (6)	37799	48581	59367
Less Cost of Goods Sold (7)	8820	11340	13860
Gross Profit	28959	37241	45507
Less Expenses			
Salaries (8)	10500	10500	10500
Payroll Taxes (9)	1575	1575	1575
Property Taxes (10)	2512	2512	2512
Insurance (11)	1950	1950	1950
Advertising and Signs	3000	3000	3000
Office Expense and Supplies	300	300	300
Telephone (12)	600	600	600
Utilities Elec. (13)	2470	2890	3310
Utilities Water (14)	1288	1456	1624
Maintenance-Bldg & Ground, Trash	200	200	200
Maintenance Pool	1000	1000	1000
Maintenance Roads	300	300	300
Depreciation (15)	7610	7610	7610
All other expenses	2500	2500	2500
Total Expenses	35805	36393	36981
Income Before Debt Service and Taxes	(6846)	848	8526

4	5	6	7	8	9	10	11	12
FIFTY (50) SITE PARK OCCUPANCY LEVEL			SIXTY (60) SITE PARK OCCUPANCY LEVEL			ONE HUNDRED (100) PARK SITES OCCUPANCY LEVEL		
35%	45%	55%	35%	45%	55%	35%	45%	55%
3675	4725	5775	4410	5670	6930	7350	9450	11550
25725	33075	40425	30870	39690	48510	51540	66150	80850
1286	1654	2022	1544	1985	2426	2573	3308	4043
1838	2363	2888	2205	2835	3465	3675	4725	5775
18375	23625	28875	22050	28350	34650	36750	47250	57750
47224	60717	74210	56669	72860	89051	94448	121433	148418
11025	14175	17325	13230	17010	20790	22050	28350	34650
36199	46542	56886	43439	55850	68261	72398	93083	113768
10500	10500	10500	10500	10500	10500	15750	15750	15750
1575	1575	1575	1575	1575	1575	2363	2363	2363
2723	2723	2723	2932	2932	2932	4200	4200	4200
2160	2160	2160	2370	2370	2370	3225	3225	3225
3000	3000	3000	3000	3000	3000	3000	3000	3000
300	300	300	300	300	300	300	300	300
600	600	600	600	600	600	600	600	600
2838	3363	3888	3205	3835	4465	4675	5725	6775
1435	1645	1855	1582	1834	2086	2170	2590	3010
200	200	200	200	200	200	200	200	200
1000	1000	1000	1000	1000	1000	1000	1000	1000
300	300	300	300	300	300	300	300	300
8100	8100	8100	8390	8390	8390	9800	9800	9800
2500	2500	2500	2500	2500	2500	2500	2500	2500
37231	37966	38701	38454	39336	40218	50083	51553	53023
(1032)	8576	18184	4985	16514	28043	22315	41530	60745

TABLE 8

SIXTY SPACE RECREATIONAL VEHICLE PARK

PRO FORMA INCOME PROJECTIONS

	1979	1980	1981	1982	1983
Gross Income					
Space Rents*	$ 5,670	$ 5,922	$ 6,174	$ 6,552	$ 6,930
Extra Occupancy	39,690	43,800	48,500	54,700	61,000
Vending Machines and Laundry	1,985	2,191	2,425	2,735	3,050
Store Sales**	2,835	2,961	3,087	3,276	3,465
	28,350	31,185	34,304	37,734	41,507
Total Income	72,860	80,137	88,316	98,445	109,022
Less Cost of Goods Sold	17,010	18,711	20,582	22,640	24,904
Gross Profit	$55,850	$61,412	$67,734	$75,805	$84,118
Less Expenses***					
Salaries	$10,500	$11,200	$11,800	$12,500	$13,250
Payroll Taxes	1,575	1,670	1,770	1,875	2,000
Property Taxes	2,932	2,932	2,932	2,932	2,932
Insurance	2,370	2,500	2,500	2,650	2,650
Advertising and Signs	3,000	3,200	3,500	3,900	4,000
Office ExpenseSupplies	300	320	350	380	420
Telephone	600	600	660	725	800
Utilities—Elec.	3,835	3,961	4,087	4,276	4,465
Utilities—Water	1,834	1,884	1,934	2,010	2,086

Maint.—Bldg. and Grounds	200	200	210	210	210
Maint.—Pool	1,000	1,060	1,125	1,200	1,275
Maint.—Roads	300	300	320	320	320
Depreciation	8,390	8,390	8,390	8,390	8,390
All Other	2,500	2,500	2,500	2,500	2,500
Total Expenses	39,336	40,717	42,078	43,868	45,298
Net Operationg Income before taxes and debt service	$16,514	$20,695	$25,656	$31,937	$38,820

*Rents will grow at a rate of about 6.0% per year. Occupancy level through better management and market growth will increase 2.0 percent per year in 1980 and 1981 and 3.0% per year in 1982 and 1983.

**Store sales will increase 10.0% per year

***Selected expenses will increase 6.0 to 10.0% per year.

TABLE 9

Return on Investment Calculations

	First Year	Fifth Year
A. Income Tax Schedule		
1. Net Operating Income	$16,514	$38,820
2. Deduct Interest on Mortgage*	14,080	12,716
3. Income Subject to Tax	2,434	26,104
4. Tax (Assume 3%)	.3	.3
5. Income Taxes	730	7,831
B. Cash Flow Schedule		
1. Net Operating Income	16,514	38,820
2. Add Back Depreciation	8,390	8,390
3. Balance	24,904	47,210
4. Deduct Mortgage Payment	16,077	16,077
5. Deduct Income Taxes	730	7,831
6. Net Cash Flow	8,087	23,302
C. Return on Investment		
1. Initial Investment	55,000	55,000
2. Add equity build up from Mortgage	0	12,400
3. Total Investment	55,000	67,400
4. Return on Investment— Net cash flow, total	14.7%	34.7%

*11.0% interest rate, original principal of 128,000; paid down to 115,600 at the end of the fifth year

182

ANALYSIS OF EXISTING PARK FOR SALE

Two RV Parks are for sale in the Cat Lake Area: The Yogi Bear Jelly-stone Park (60 units for $650,000) and Jim John's Trailer Park (39 units for $165,000). Price eliminates Jellystone from consideration. Following is an analysis of the Jim John Property.

A 39-space combination mobile-recreational vehicle park is on the market in the Hickory Creek area. The asking price is $165,000. Following is an evaluation of this park as an alternative to developing a new park:

A. Owners Income Statement

B. Price and Cost Analysis

C. Reconstructed Income Statement

D. Return on Investment Analysis

A. Owner's Income State (Unaudited—available from Real Estate Broker)*

Income

Space Rents (25)	8,142	
Mobile Home Rental	10,388	
Misc.	180	
TOTAL INCOME		18,710

LESS EXPENSES

Utilities	6,332	
Auto Expense	1,242	
Office Supplies	234	
Laundry	82	
Travel	106	
Maintenance	2,064	
Units Supplies	664	
Advertising	1,142	
Taxes	1,598	
Other	32	
Total Expenses		13,496
Net Operating Income		5,214

*Income and Expense date annualized from a 6 month's statement for the period ending June 30, 1978.

An evaluation of "Jim John's trailer park" includes the following: RV space rents for $4.00 per night. Based on a 210-day season (7 months), the $8,142 reported represents a 25% occupancy level. Such a low performance can be attributed to a low amenity, low price marketing strategy. Since the overall market demand in the Hickory Creek area is strong and increasing,* this strategy is missing the market that wants more amenities and are willing to pay for them. Therefore any consideration of this existing park should be from the standpoint of adding sufficient quality and quantity of amenities to increase market penetration and hence the occupancy level.

The second income item, mobile home rentals provides a stabilizing and positive element in this investment opportunity. The $10,388 breaks down exactly. Nevertheless, the year round nature of this source of income has some definite advantages.

A review of the expenses shows them to be lacking in salaries, insurance, and advertising (low), telephone utilities seem to be quite high and should be checked out. Following is a reconstructed income statement reflecting an increase in investment (amenities).

B. Price and Cost Analysis

The Jim John's Trailer Park is offered for sale for $165,000. Using a gross capitalization rate in the range of 13% to 15%, a counter offer in the range of $125,000 to $145,000 is appropriate. Assume the high end of the value range—$145,000. The following amenities need to be constructed.

_____

*Based on Canton Corps of Engineers Studies in 1972 and 1977.

184

Recreation Room and Store (1000 sq. ft.)	$ 20,000
Restroom and Laundry	8,000
Tables, Grills and Playground	4,500
Swimming and Wading Pools	14,000
Total Additional Investment	$ 46,500
Add Purchase Price, say	145,000
	$191,500

C. Reconstructed First Year Income Statement

Income:

Space Rents (45% occupancy @ $7.00)	$ 25,800
MH pad rentals (10 pads @ 70% occupancy)	7,140
MH units rentals 3 units @ $200.00	7,200
Store Sales—RV campers	14,700
Store Sales—MH units ($50.00/mo.)	6,000
Total Income	$ 60,840
Less Cost of Goods Sold	12,420
Gross Profit	$ 48,420
Less Expenses (See Table Column 1)	35,805
Net Operating Profit	$ 12,615

D. Return on Investment Analysis

Net Operating Profit	$ 12,615
Add Back Depreciation	7,610
Subtotal	20,225
Less Income Taxes (30% Tax Bracket)	0
Less Debt Service (11.0%, 20 yr. mtg.)	17,772
Net Cash Flow	$ 2,453

Using similar economic and financial data as shown in Table 9, this alternative of purchasing an existing RV park produces greater net cash flow than the comparable newly constructed park (458 for 40 units, 45% occupancy level). More favorable seller financing for part of the purchased park would also enhance the return on investment. Of course, additional land is available for development. Increasing the number of RV spaces to 50 or 60 will greatly increase the profitability of this investment opportunity.

The above has been presented to give the reader an idea of how to analyze the purchase alternative. A different amenity or added spaces scheme might prove to be more financially feasible should investment funds be tight.

APPENDIX A

Recreational Vehicles Shipments

Year	Total Shipments	Total Trailers**	Truck Campers	Camping Trailers	Motor Homes	Pickup Covers
1977	745,600**	167,900	31,900	53,900	280,200*	211,700
1976	756,300*	189,700	42,000	53,300	256,100*	215,200
1975	552,000	150,600	44,300	48,100	96,600	211,500
1974	529,000	126,300	45,400	55,200	68,900	233,400
1973	752,500	212,300	89,800	97,700	129,000	223,700
1972	747,500	250,800	105,100	110,200	116,800	164,600
1971	549,400	190,800	107,200	95,800	57,200	98,400
1970	472,000	138,000	95,900	116,110	30,300	91,700
1969	514,100	144,000	92,500	141,000	23,100	113,500
1968	483,100	115,200	79,500	125,200	13,200	150,000
1967	244,430	94,500	61,600	79,280	9,050	N.A.
1966	219,810	87,300	54,500	72,300	5,710	N.A.
1965	192,830	76,600	44,300	67,220	4,710	N.A.
1964	151,000	64,200	34,800	52,000	N.A.	N.A.
1963	118,600	51,500	26,800	40,300	N.A.	N.A.
1962	80,300	40,600	16,700	23,000	N.A.	N.A.
1961	62,600	28,800	15,800	18,000	N.A.	N.A.

*Not comparable with previous years. Includes 100,000 vans with minimum life support systems (surfer vans) in 1976 and 120,000 in 1977.

**Includes 12,600 5th wheel type travel trailers in 1974, 16,600 in 1975, 21,400 in 1976, and 22,000 in 1977.

N.A. Not Available

Source: Recreation Vehicle Industry Association

APPENDIX B

LITTLE ROCK DISTRICT
CORPS OF ENGINEERS
PROJECT VISITATION

Visitation (1)

Project	1959	1960	1961	1962
Beaver	—	—	—	—
Blue Mountain	286,800	265,300	296,100	355,106
Bull Shoals	2,721,300	2,581,100	2,060,300	2,191,850
Clearwater	460,000	414,600	479,800	541,213
Dardanelle	—	—	—	—
Greers Ferry	—	—	—	—
Nimrod	273,300	320,000	345,900	312,060
Norfolk	1,080,000	1,121,000	1,151,500	1,202,326
Table Rock	—	2,407,900	3,360,900	3,501,145
Total	4,821,400	7,109,900	7,694,500	8,103,700

Visitation (1)

Project	1949	1950	1951	1952
Blue Mountain	120,996	121,737	160,543	182,452
Bull Shoals	—	—	—	412,818
Clearwater	108,620	139,469	224,959	165,159
Nimrod	454,509	116,739	163,512	227,556
Norfolk	454,509	559,878	742,364	831,594
Total	778,964	937,823	1,291,378	1,819,579

Note: (1) Visitation is expressed in recreation days. A recreation day is defined as the attendance of one person at the project and engaging in one or more recreational activities for one day or a fraction thereof.

LITTLE ROCK DISTRICT
CORPS OF ENGINEERS
PROJECT VISITATION

Visitation (1)

1963	1964	1965	1966	1967	1968
—	—	548,200	1,536,000	1,687,900	1,781,800
431,900	429,300	255,200	146,000	228,300	211,800
2,730,000	2,249,600	2,137,800	1,992,600	1,974,000	2,781,300
474,100	483,400	549,700	473,700	603,700	608,900
—	—	1,588,800	1,318,100	1,216,900	1,033,600
912,000	1,400,200	1,428,400	1,431,000	1,631,000	2,006,600
324,800	334,800	325,500	357,400	410,500	434,800
1,230,400	1,486,500	1,504,200	1,533,500	1,531,500	1,767,100
3,258,900	2,872,300	3,331,660	3,217,000	3,377,000	3,931,800
9,362,100	9,256,100	11,669,400	12,005,300	12,660,800	14,557,700

Visitation (1)

1953	1954	1955	1956	1957	1958
204,871	216,079	214,000	196,800	254,900	254,700
790,923	1,107,925	1,548,000	1,663,000	1,765,000	2,693,000
189,347	225,079	280,000	296,000	434,000	493,000
223,308	230,847	230,000	235,000	229,000	248,600
749,442	693,070	850,000	893,000	935,000	1,090,400
2,157,891	2,473,000	3,122,000	3,283,800	3,617,900	4,779,700

LITTLE ROCK DISTRICT
CORPS OF ENGINEERS
PROJECT VISITATION

Visitation (1)

Project	1969	1970	1971	1972
Beaver	2,040,900	2,088,100	2,341,600	2,989,000
Blue Mountain	440,300	411,700	555,200	402,200
Bull Shoals	3,156,800	3,397,900	3,959,200	3,939,700
Clearwater	718,100	748,600	795,500	847,400
Greers Ferry	2,207,000	2,741,500	3,038,800	3,598,700
Nimrod	500,600	466,600	472,200	44,100
Norfork	2,099,500	2,487,100	2,930,100	3,185,500
Table Rock	4,876,800	6,084,200	5,552,900	6,328,300
Subtotal (Lakes)	16,040,000	18,425,700	19,645,500	21,734,900
Dardanelle	1,276,700	1,538,900	1,880,000	1,759,300
Ozark	—	—	235,100	431,400
Norell L&D	79,300	66,200	107,700	166,000
L&D 2	323,600	360,000	511,800	618,500
L&D 3	93,500	155,300	172,300	227,300
L&D 4	205,900	223,700	468,000	579,200
L&D 5	91,000	172,000	209,700	275,600
David D. Terry	234,000	288,600	404,300	550,400
Murray L&D	—	—	251,000	183,200
Toad Suck Ferry	—	—	63,400	63,300
L&D 9	—	—	75,500	91,700
L&D 13	—	—	188,100	282,400
Subtotal (Ark. River)	2,304,000	2,824,700	4,566,900	5,228,300
DISTRICT TOTAL	18,344,000	21,250,400	24,212,400	26,963,200

NOTES: (1) Visitation is expressed in recreation days. A recreation day is
defined as the attendance of one person at the project and engaging in one or more recreational activities for one day or a fraction
thereof.

LITTLE ROCK DISTRICT
CORPS OF ENGINEERS
PROJECT VISITATION

Visitation (1)

1973	1974	1975	1976	1977
3,227,000	3,478,500	3,179,000	3,842,400	3,558,100
265,000	262,400	245,800	223,300	232,200
3,066,300	3,695,300	4,385,700	3,885,400	3,595,800
816,600	895,800	911,200	946,000	810,400
3,419,900	3,423,600	3,663,700	4,224,100	4,238,700
514,100	493,500	494,400	494,800	439,900
2,984,400	3,197,100	3,592,700	3,263,700	3,235,100
5,754,800	5,591,000	6,188,100	6,379,200	6,393,500
20,048,100	21,037,200	22,660,600	23,258,900	22,413,700
2,128,400	2,325,700	2,217,900	2,778,300	3,259,000
490,900	580,600	620,300	860,000	953,100
54,300	74,800	69,000	67,500	36,400
547,300	568,300	512,800	639,400	488,400
190,600	186,000	225,600	230,700	230,600
688,600	593,800	603,600	615,200	196,800
342,700	259,300	296,000	255,300	176,400
638,900	398,100	641,200	823,500	1,570,300
387,200	402,400	546,500	811,100	819,400
71,000	134,400	264,100	530,000	540,500
150,800	136,700	176,600	353,700	345,100
184,400	198,500	504,800	599,000	675,100
5,875,100	5,858,600	6,678,400	8,563,700	9,291,100
25,923,200	26,895,800	29,339,000	31,822,600	31,704,800

RECREATIONAL VISITATION DATA
LITTLE ROCK DISTRICT
ESTIMATED DISTRIBUTION OF VISITATION AS OF DECEMBER 1972

Park	Total Visits to Park Jan–Dec.	Boating	Fishing	Hunting
Blue Springs	93,389	10,499	47,056	0
Dam Site North	51,044	5,248	27,587	0
Dam Site South	102,011	10,536	54,805	0
Hickory Creek	199,879	19,942	109,342	0
Horseshoe Bend	145,004	14,727	79,122	0
Indian Creek	19,112	1,849	9,471	0
Lost Bridge	115,154	11,843	62,515	0
Dan and App Works	39,643	3,852	21,844	0
Prairie Creek	308,468	30,834	169,525	0
Rocky Branch	98,007	7,988	59,839	0
Starkey	33,595	4,619	20,403	0
Ventris	6,085	0,635	3,312	0
War Eagle	53,329	5,327	29,629	0
Unimproved Access	1,553,950	140,787	872,819	0
Launch Complexes	42,428	3,397	24,291	0
Overlook	108,494	0	0	0
Walk in Visitors	19,350	0	11,099	0
TOTAL	2,989,009	271,996	1,602,559	0

RECREATIONAL VISITATION DATA
LITTLE ROCK DISTRICT
ESTIMATED DISTRIBUTION OF VISITATION AS OF DECEMBER 1972

Picknicking	Sightseeing	Skiing	Swimming	Camping	Other
16,251	30,581	2,846	12,192	4,128	511
7,002	13,446	1,460	13,987	15,377	149
14,006	26,305	2,918	28,242	30,899	260
27,125	55,888	5,515	52,213	59,055	650
19,814	39,537	4,109	38,822	43,210	494
2,352	2,954	579	9,809	7,427	69
15,805	30,616	3,331	31,448	34,595	375
5,330	11,563	1,057	9,950	11,539	130
41,918	86,878	8,585	80,454	90,933	1,125
4,297	22,406	3,474	16,713	27,739	2,504
5,407	6,939	1,351	10,857	10,587	115
841	1,599	180	1,689	1,836	23
7,256	15,301	1,503	13,771	15,606	239
203,855	501,873	37,721	349,434	343,671	5,501
5,336	15,558	852	7,866	11,199	128
0	108,494	0	0	0	0
2,459	6,980	0	3,728	0	70
378,942	976,960	75,408	681,122	707,708	12,329

RECREATIONAL VISITATION DATA
LITTLE ROCK DISTRICT
ESTIMATED DISTRIBUTION OF VISITATION

Project-Beaver Lake

Park	Total Visits to Park Jan–Dec	Boating	Fishing	Hunting
Blue Springs	77,170	15,307	32,567	0
Dam Site North	183,443	32,132	74,265	216
Dam Site South	140,863	24,315	56,425	303
Hickory Creek	286,981*	43,278*	44,951	0
Horseshoe Bend	170,684	25,796	26,774	0
Indian Creek	25,765	2,242	6,678	57
Lost Bridge	120,581	35,780	49,290	127
Dam and App Works	75,553	4,810	43,121	0
Prairie Creek	520,611*	80,861*	76,034	0
Rocky Branch	89,849	29,118	37,106	0
Starkey	48,109	14,754	20,097	0
Ventris	8,025	807	2,122	0
War Eagle	69,536	20,740	30,198	0
Other Access Areas	1,544,474	298,136	836,669	96,854
Launch Complexes	67,844	12,185	36,824	217
Overlook	95,873	0	0	0
Walk in visitors	32,715	893	18,964	236
TOTAL	3,558,070	641,076	1,392,004	97,900

RECREATIONAL VISITATION DATA
LITTLE ROCK DISTRICT
ESTIMATED DISTRIBUTION OF VISITATION

Project-Bever Lake

Picnicing	Sightseeing	Skiing	Swimming	Camping	Other
5,313	22,461	4,914	33,540	40,399	0
16,278	47,086	16,183	111,045	96,844	0
13,666	37,445	12,574	85,070	74,774	0
79,736	69,376	32,650	134,578	84,515*	0
47,422	25,740	19,543	80,469	54,533	0
4,523	9,456	1,631	8,823	12,022	0
12,491	29,382	11,455	56,984	63,632	0
5,507	28,904	1,180	12,193	0	12,587
152,155	123,544	57,672	243,309	163,116*	0
10,058	20,982	7,875	41,012	46,301	0
5,495	11,750	4,349	21,614	24,611	0
1,373	2,787	516	2,692	4,721	0
9,031	17,915	6,130	28,688	33,908	0
88,485	610,001	61,788	410,015	0	202,251
4,139	26,368	2,554	17,446	0	9,462
0	95,873	0	0	0	0
1,680	14,327	0	3,720	0	0
457,280	1,193,318	240,956	1,291,158	699,310	224,294

APPENDIX C

FACT SHEET
EXPLAINING HOW TO FILE AN APPLICATION
FOR AN SBA LOAN UNDER THE GUARANTY PLAN

How does the Guaranty Plan Work?

The Guaranty Plan makes it possible for you to file an application for a loan direct with your bank at a reasonable interest rate, providing the following facts exist and use of proceeds are for eligible purposes:

1. That your relationship and credit standing is good with your bank

2. That the loan applied for can be secured with collateral now and to be purchased from the proceeds of the loan and considered by bank to be adequate to reasonably secure the loan.

3. That the balance sheet shows the net worth of your existing business or the new business to be established in an approximate amount equal to the amount of the loan requested, and that the rate of indebtedness to net worth is not considered excessive.

4. That your past operating statements of your existing business show the ability to retire the loan from earnings or, in the case of a new business, that a three-year projection of earnings will show necessary profits to retire the loans.

5. That your past records of handling obligations with the bank and other business firms with whom you are dealing is satisfactory.

6. That you and any officers of your corporation have not been adjudicated a bankrupt, or connected with a receivership, or involved in any criminal or subversive activities, or other legal proceedings of a detrimental nature.

7. If you have an existing business, we will need a balance sheet not over ninety days old and operating statements for the past three years. If it is a business to be purchased, we will need the reason for selling, copies of income tax returns on the business for the past three years, and a personal balance sheet not over ninety days old on you as the applicant.

If it is a new business to be established, we will need a pro form balance sheet on the business and a three-year projection of earnings.

With the above information, we would like an opportunity to assist you in presenting you application to your bank of account in good form. There is no charge for our services.

What is meant by a long term commitment?

If the collateral offered to secure the loan is of a long lasting nature, such as land and buildings, a maximum period of fifteen years can be considered on new construction and ten years on existing building.

If the loan is for working capital, inventory, machinery or equipment, etc., the term generally will be five years, with a maximum of six years.

Further Information

The most valuable asset a borrower can have is good established bank credit. Any supplier seeking credit information contacts your bank. SBA helps you establish this credit.

It is felt that you should know the majority of the banks in Oklahoma are familiar with the Guaranty Plan. If your application has merit and is considered a feasible application, the bank will usually give consideration to submission of your application to their discount committee, when it is properly prepared.

We will process your application in approximately fifteen days after it is received, depending on our backlog at the time.

Minimum bank participation is 10% or the amount of present indebtedness to the bank, whichever is greater.

PROCEDURE TO FOLLOW

1. Assemble the information outlined below.

2. Take it to your bank and ask your banker to review the information and loan proposal. (As we have no direct funds, it will be necessary for you to locate a bank that is willing to participate with SBA and make the loan).

3. If the bank is willing to participate, ask the bank to forward the information to us for our review, along with their comments.

INFORMATION NEEDED FOR LOAN REVIEW

1. Brief resume of business

2. Brief resume of management setting forth prior business experience technical training, education, age, health, etc.

3. Itemized use of loan proceeds:

Working Capital	$_____
Land	$_____
Building	$_____
Furniture and Fixtures	$_____
Machinery and Equipment	$_____
Automotive Equipment	$_____
Other	$_____
TOTAL	$_____

4. Current business balance sheet and profit/loss statement.

5. Year ending business balance sheets and profit/loss statements for the last three years or if the business has been in existence less than three years, furnish the financial statements for each year it has been in operation. (Copies of the financial statements submitted with the income tax returns are adequate.)

6. If the business is not in existence, but is proposed, furnish a projected balance sheet of the business showing its proposed assets, liabilities and net worth upon commencement of operations, together with projected annual operating statements for the first two years of operation.

7. Furnish a separate personal balance sheet showing all assets owned and liabilities owed outside of the business.

The above is the information a Loan Officer will need to properly analyze your loan proposal.

FEASIBILITY STUDY

HEALTH-CARE ADMINISTRATION PROGRAM

School of Business

Fairfield University

Fairfield, U.S.A.

Prepared by

Robert E. Stevens, Ph.D.
Philip K. Sherwood, Ed.D.

STEVENS-SHERWOOD AND ASSOCIATES
2140 S. 78th E. Ave.
Tulsa, Oklahoma

CERTIFICATION

We hereby certify that we have no interest, present or contemplated, in the proposed Fairfield University Care Program and that to the best of our knowledge and belief, the statements and information contained in this report are correct—subject to the limitations herein set forth.

Robert E. Stevens, Ph.D.

Philip K. Sherwood, Ed.D.

TABLE OF CONTENTS

EXECUTIVE SUMMARY

Purpose

The purpose of the Master's of Business Administration Concentration in Health-Care Administration (HCA) is to produce competent administrators for management in the rapidly growing health-care field. This study recommends the establishment of the HCA program at Fairfield University.

Environment

The environment and statistics show that the health-care industry is expanding world-wide and that the capital expenditures in the field are increasing dramatically. It is the second largest industry in the country in terms of expenditures and accounts for an estimated ten percent or more of our GNP. Government and private forecasters are predicting as many as 100,000 new jobs by 1985.

Locally, the Fairfield area has five major hospitals and the soon-to-be operational University Hospital. The demand and need for a health-care administration program appears to be strong worldwide, in Fairfield, and perhaps most dramatically here at the huge University Medical complex.

*THERE IS SUFFICIENT DEMAND FOR HEALTH CARE ADMINIS-TRATORS TO WARRANT THE PROPOSED PROJECT.

Strengths and Weaknesses

An analysis of the strengths and weaknesses indicates that the Fairfield University School of Business is well able to build the new health-care program on the strong foundation of its MBA program. Joined with support and

206

resources from the Schools of Medicine, Dentistry, Nursing, Law, and staff from the University Medical Complex, Fairfield University has the ingredients for a successful and complete master's program in health-care administration.

There are some potential weaknesses. The University is young and has had only about twenty years to build its reputation and upgrade the quality of its programs. The Medical and Dental schools may be completely absorbed in securing accreditation and by the demands of rapid expansion, limiting time for contribution to the health-care administration program. Another important consideration is the effect of transfer students from the MBA to the MHCA program to the detriment of the MBA.

*THE RESOURCES AT FAIRFIELD UNIVERSITY ARE SUFFICIENT TO WARRANT THE ESTABLISHMENT OF THE PROGRAM

Assumptions

There are enough MBA candidates at Fairfield University interested in health-care to justify the program. The demand for administrative people in health-care will increase. The insufficiency of internship positions in the University Medical Complex will necessitate affiliation with other health-related institutions.

*THERE WILL BE A SUFFICIENT SUPPLY OF STUDENTS FOR THE HCA PROGRAM.

Benefit/Cost Analysis

The analysis of costs and benefits reveals a slight deficit in the first year of operation. However, the amount is only 2.8% of the costs of the program. Often non-monetary benefits far outweigh the small incremental cost involved in establishing the program. The intangible benefits cause the program to be favorable.

*THE BENEFIT/COST ANALYSIS JUSTIFIES THE PROGRAM.

Objectives

The objectives for instituting the program are the graduation of 15 MHCA's May, 1983; enrollment of 10 students in Health Care I (HCI) for fall 1982, 20 students in HCI for spring 1983, and 20 students in HCII for fall 1983; establishment of 5+ internships for summer 1983; sending Dr. Jones to health-care marketing conference; helping Dr. Cappelli get HCII ready for summer; preparing Dr. Jones to teach HCIII in spring 1983; and the recruitment of faculty for HCIV in spring 1984.

Strategy Summary

The strategy to establish the Health-Care Administration program will be to maximize the benefits of the strengths outlined in the report and minimizing and anticipating the effects of the weaknesses. Coverage support from the University publications, seminars, and University public relations will be pursued. Long-range planning and financing are outlined in the full report.

*THE LONG-RANGE BENEFITS OF ESTABLISHING THE PROGRAM APPEAR EXTREMELY POSITIVE. IN THE LONG-RANGE VIEW, THE PROGRAM IS PROJECTED TO BREAK EVEN AND PROVIDE BENEFIT AND SUPPORT TO THE MEDICAL AND HEALING MISSION OF THE UNIVERSITY.

CHAPTER 1

INTRODUCTION

Purpose

The purpose of the Master's of Business Administration Concentration in Health-Care Administration (HCA) is to produce competent administrators for management in the rapidly growing health-care field. This study will focus on the feasibility of such a program. This will involve an assessment of the supply of potential students, the need for health-care administrators, the benefit/cost relationship of providing the program, the current faculty resources, the availability of new faculty, and the need for new library resources.

Preliminary Assumptions

Several basic assumptions were made in generating the information and in analyzing the data for this report. These assumptions are important in understanding the conclusions stated in the last section of the report.

Assumptions About Future Events

The first assumption we made in proposing this program was that there will be enough MBA candidates at Fairfield University interested in health-care administration to justify estalishing the program. Because of the possible demands of the program, it is necessary that admission initially be restricted to undergraduate business majors. We did have ten students take Health Care I in the fall and 17 enroll for the spring semester. Not all will be Health-Care Administration majors, however.

A second assumption is that the demand for management people in the nation's health-care services industry will increase. The environmental analysis cited earlier gives some indication of the extent to which we can rely on such growth. Another relevant consideration is the likelihood of federal legislation for national health-care cost containment. According to the Center for Research in Ambulatory Care Administration, "Most experts in the health-care administration field agree that national health insurance will become available to all Americans within the next seven years or so." Such programs would produce many new job openings for health administrators with the federal agencies regulating their implementation.

A third assumption is that once the University Medical Complex has opened, it will be able to generate adequate patient revenue. Failure to do so would probably cause a loss of internship positions, among many other effects.

Our fourth assumption has a related concern. The University Medical Complex alone cannot be expected to provide sufficient internship positions. It is necessary, therefore, to maintain and develop affiliations with other hospitals, health-care facilities, and planning agencies. It is assumed that internships will be available not only in the University Medical Complex and FU-related clinics, but also in other health centers, such as St. Mary's.

Finally, it is assumed that this Health Care major program can be carried out with minimal additional cost to the University. The largest expected cost is the salary for one full-time faculty member at the assistant professor's or associate professor's level. We were unable to find the right person in our recruiting efforts. Dean J. Charles Smith will guide the program, utilizing our own graduate faculty and adjunct professors.

CHAPTER II

MARKET POTENTIAL

Environmental Analysis

The health-care industry is rapidly growing in America and abroad. In 1973, more than $1 billion was spent on new hospital construction in the United States; in 1974, this figure increased by $238 million to $1,240,000,000. In that year there were already 7,174 hospitals with a total of 1,512,689 beds serving 35,506,190 in-patients (out-patient figures are not available). In addition, 12,871 nursing homes (1973) were serving 824,038 patients and employing 567,717 full-time personnel.

National health expenditures increased from 4.6% of our gross national product in 1950 to 7.7% of a much larger GNP in 1975. Today that figure approaches 10%, according to Donald Clark, labor economist at the Division of Manpower and Occupational Outlook, U.S. Bureau of Labor.

These figures indicate that the health-care industry is already large and is growing rapidly. Opportunities abound for health-care administrators, such as those to be trained by the master's program. U.S. News & World Report in its January 3, 1977 issue, predicted 100,000 new jobs in health-care administration by 1985. This means the field could increase in size by 66% over the present 150,000 jobs in just eight years. Perhaps a more reliable view is given by the Division of Manpower in predicting the growth to increase from 160,000 in 1976 to 232,000 in 1985. The number stands at 180,000 positions in 1978, far greater than the estimated 29,000 degree-holders in the field by 1980. Opportunities in the field have broadened beyond hospital administration to include the areas of health planning centers, government regulatory agencies, health-maintenance organizations, health-care consulting firms, mental health services, health insurance agencies, public health, and long-term nursing home care. This is a firm indication of the great need for programs to train these administrators.

Turning from the nation-wide job market for graduates to the local climate for training students, we find very favorable conditions. The Fairfield area presently has five major hospitals: St. Peter's, St. Mary's, Childrens, Woodview, and County General. The addition of the University Medical Complex hospital adjoining the University with its planned 294, and eventual 777 beds, plus an enormous out-patient clinic, and research facility will make Fairfield an excellent city for training future hospital administrators. The University retirement area adjacent to the University campus and local nursing homes also will provide opportunities for students to meet and work with medical personnel involved with long-term nursing home care.

The demand for a health-care administration program also comes from within the University. At least six MBA graduates have gone into health-related fields, and several current MBA students are likely to pursue health administration careers. In the Economics I classes, a disguised survey revealed that 30 students were definitely interested in hospital administration. Much of this interest is generated by the University Medical Complex under construction and the growing emphasis on quality health care in the United States.

The various schools and departments at Fairfield University also constitute important environmental factors. Most important, of course, is the School of Business which will be offering the new degree.

The University presently offers a Master of Business Administration degree which provides training in management strategy and techniques, long-range planning/management by objectives, organizational behavior, and other aspects of business. Most of the courses required for the master's health-care administration are identical to those already required for the MBA program. Students in the degree program have full use of the school's resources and benefit from the association with business students and faculty in other specialized disciplines.

Other students of major importance are the School of Medicine and the School of Dentistry which opened in 1978, both of whose faculty adjuncts additional School of Business faculty could teach the remainder of the courses for the health-care administration degree. The program will not only give business-degree candidates specialized knowledge about problems in health services, but will also afford them an opportunity to learn how to relate to medically-oriented persons. Simultaneously, the courses should give some medical and dental students a chance to become acquainted with the kinds of people with whom they will be dealing in the business aspects of their profession.

The University School of Nursing is another valuable resource for health-care administration education. Relations with nursing personnel are vital to hospital administration. Graduates of this baccalaureate and master's nursing program have a basic degree in professional nursing and are prepared to take State Board examinations for licensure as registered nurses.

Finally, the Fairfield School of Law enables health-care administration students to have access to faculty familiar with the kinds of legal problems encountered in the medical services. The School of Business might be offering the JD/MBA degree with the School of Law in the fall of 1983.

These graduate and undergraduate programs offered by Fairfield University in conjunction with the other schools now on campus provide a complete educational milieu for a master's program in health-care administration.

Other schools offering the Health-Care major:

	Typical Program Length		Number of Health Related Courses	Research Project or Thesis
	Didactic	Field Exp.		
University of Chicago	18 mos.	Concurrent	6	No
Cornell University	18 mos.	3 mos.	5	No
University of Pennsylvania (Wharton School)	18 mos.	3 mos.	NA	Yes
Northwestern University	18 mos.	3 mos.	5 w/ additional speciali- zation	No
University of Oklahoma	36 hrs.	No	3	Yes
Washington University	18 mos.	Optional	NA	Yes
University of Wisconsin- Madison	18 mos.	3 mos.	NA	No
St. Louis University	18 mos.	3 mos.	4	No
University of Cincinnati	12 mos.	9 mos.	NA	Optional
Harvard University	18 mos.	3 mos.	NA	Yes

Strengths and Weaknesses

One of the major strengths of this proposal is that two-thirds of the present courses in the MBA program will be used as a foundation for the program in health-care administration. The Business School faculty is already well established at Fairfield and their experience and the excellent reputation the School has for placing its graduates will provide a strong foundation for the proposed specialized degree. The thesis requirement in the program will provide for further specialization according to the individual student's interest.

The University has outstanding educational facilities which are available to candidates for the degree. The Learning Resources Center, having been enlarged to accommodate the Schools of Medicine, Dentistry, and Law, is fully equipped with a Dial Access Information Retrieval System, auto-tutorial science laboratories, and a cassette language laboratory.

Having Schools of Dentistry, Law, Medicine, and Nursing on the same campus is, of course, an important strength of the new program. Many universities offering degrees in health-care administration do not have these related schools. This inter-disciplinary nature is enhanced by the concept of cross-pollination and healing team preparation which is emerging into the academic process of the University.

One of the most notable strengths of the program comes from the University Medical Complex hospital adjoining the campus along with the dental and medical clinics. These facilities are important parts in providing a complete holistic approach to medical care. The University Medical Complex brings visibility to the program within the organization, a feature other programs rarely enjoy. Many of the graduates of this program have internship training opportunities in the University Medical Complex and clinics, and thus they receive excellent preparation for future employment. The clinic management exposure is particularly important, as trends indicate growth in medical group and health maintenance organization management. Significantly enough, there are no programs in the United States now that sufficiently educate in this area.

The final and most important strength of the program is the solid reputation of Fairfield University as a institution of higher learning founded on a clear and positive mission related to the whole person and a holistic approach to medicine.

One of the weaknesses of the program is the youth of the University. FU opened in the early 1960's and thus has had only around 20 years in which to build its reputation and upgrade the quality of its programs.

There are several problems involved with the Medical and Dental schools which inhibit use of their faculty and staff to teach in the new program. One facing the Medical School is securing accreditation. This will be a full-time consideration for both the clinical and administrative personnel of the school until after full accreditation is received sometime after 1982. Another problem is that the 1978 class size of 50 is expected to double in 1982 after the first class graduates. This again means a considerable load on the medical faculty to prepare for expansion. The faculty of the Schools of Medicine and Dentistry have an additional problem of developing private and hospital practices in the Fairfield area.

The clinical specialists on the faculty will have additional problems in that (a) only a nucleus of the people involved in medical clinical education will be here prior to 1982, and (b) the clinical faculty are likely to be involved in some of the planning for the University Medical Complex.

All of these factors mean that the Medical and Dental School faculties will be pressed for time and may be unable to fully participate in other academic programs, such as the master's in health-care administration major, which would draw them away from specifically medical and dental-oriented teaching.

To be sure, some of these problems can be lessened by utilizing the services of selected administrative persons, such as Dental School Dean John W. Hoover, who are not involved in clinical demands. Another solution is to hire a full-time faculty member and utilize part-time adjunct faculty, such as R. William York and Tom Cassidy, who are now full-time administrators. There is also a reasonable probability that part-time

216

faculty may be obtainable from the Fairfield health-care community, including administrators or medical personnel.

Recent cutbacks in University programs and support services could result in sub-level enrollment. Recruitment efforts have been reduced to a response-basis where much care is taken in responding to rather than enlisting interest. The Placement and Alumni offices are important in securing results in employment which in the long run have the effect of generating students for the program.

The number of MBA students that will transfer to the MHCA program will have a good effect on the MHCA but a detrimental effect on the MBA program in terms of attrition. Thus, the addition of 20 MHCA students does not ensure the overall addition of 20 to the School of Business. Efforts must be maintained toward the accomplishment of an overall increase of 20 graduate business students.

The proposed program and the curriculum developed especially for health administration education is sharply focused. Courses involving mental health-care administration, long-term care institutions, and in the legal problems of health care, would contribute to a better preparation for students entering the job market. The top schools in health-care management, namely, Chicago (Business School), Pennsylvania (Wharton), Cornell (School of Business and Public Administration), and Northwestern (School of Management), all offer advanced seminars in their programs. Therefore, seminars will be offered to further complement the academic programs and maximize local talent and resources.

CHAPTER III

COST OF THE PROGRAM

The success of the Health-Care Administration program depends on the Benefit/Cost relationship. The following section will deal with the direct costs of the program. The incremental costs of the program will be assessed with little attempt to allocate overhead costs at this point.

The following costs have been identified as relating directly to the initial phase of the new Health-Care Administration program.

Costs

A.	Library volumes (non-recurring) 300 × $20[1] Continuing acquisitions		1,000
B.	Faculty		
	Salaries - 4 faculty ¼ time	$30,000	
	2 adjuncts	3,000	33,000
C.	Financial Aid: ⅓ X Full-time tuition ($54,810)		18,270
D.	Facilities: Excess capacity - no addition to cost		N.A.
E.	GSH depreciation: Tenants pay damages		N.A.
F.	Professional meetings:		3,000
G.	Research		5,000
H.	Addition to MBA budget: Support		10,000
			−$70,270

Notes:

1. Will be covered by a grant of $6,000. This cost is not included here.

218

Assumptions:

1. That 6 MBA students will defect to the MHCA, and that an overall increase in students would be 14, not 20.

2. That there will be 10 single students, 2 married students in furnished apartments, and 8 married students in unfurnished apartments.

The cost for 1980–81 has been:

Revenue

      Fall - 10 students at $135 hr. X 30 hours

      Spring - 17 students at $135 X 30 hours

USE OF AVAILABLE RESOURCES

Very few additional resources are needed to begin this program. Two-thirds of the courses for the new program are already available to MBA students. The specialized courses for health-care administration and core MBA courses will be taught with the existing facilities of the Business, Law, Medical, and Dental schools, use of the full-time faculty, and a couple of part-time adjunct faculty. No additional classroom space will be needed.

The University Medical Complex, University clinics, and nursing homes will provide for most of the internships required.

The library will need to stock no more than 300 new volumes at an approximate cost of $20 each.

Greater revenue will be generated from tuition and graduate housing occupancy than will be expended in increased costs. Non-economic advantages of the program are the ability of offering another program for the University which will attract more FU undergraduates, and the prospect of graduating whole persons specifically trained and educated for the health-care administration field.

CHAPTER IV
REVENUES, EXPENSES, AND BENEFITS

Purpose

The purpose of the MBA with a health-care administration major is to produce highly trained and competent administrators to provide management service for the nation's and the world's rapidly growing health-care needs.

The program provides opportunity for specialization by degree candidates in the Business School and will complement and enlarge the value of the Schools of Medicine and Dentistry and the University medical facilities. It also gives Fairfield University a more competitive graduate program, as many more graduates consider staying for careers at FU.

Moreover, persons already employed by the University may seek to improve their educational development through this specialized program.

Objectives. The specific measurable objectives for the major in health-care administration would be:

1. Enroll 15 students in May 1983.
2. Enroll 10 students for fall 1982 in Health Care I.
3. Enroll 20 students for spring 1983 in Health Care I.
4. Enroll 20 students for fall 1983 in Health Care II.
5. Establish 5+ internships for summer of 1983.
6. Send Dr. Robert E. Jones to Health Care Marketing Conference in summer 1982.

7. Help Dr. John Capelli get Health Care II ready for summer 1983.

8. Have Dr. Jones teach Health Care III in spring 1983.

9. Recruit faculty to teach Health Care IV in spring 1984.

Strategy

Our strategy to achieve these objectives will be to build on the solid base of the School of Business, Schools of Medicine and Dentistry, and the emphasis on health-care from the University Medical Complex. These efforts will gain national attention. Coverage support from the university publications, seminars, and university public relations efforts will be pursued.

Central to the health of the program is the ability to financially support the program. The following analysis for 1981–82 shows:

I. REVENUE

A.	Tuition 20 students X $135 hr. X 22 hrs/yr		$59,400	
	Part-time: Assume 5 students (2 @ 6 hrs.,			
	3 @ 3 hrs.)		+2,835	
			62,234	
	Less 6 students from MBA:[1]			
	6 X $135 X 18 hrs. =		−14,580	$47,655
B.	GSH Rent:[2] 10 stu. X $120 X 8.5 mo. =	$11,050		
	2 st. X $240 X 8.5 mo. =	4,080		
	8 stu. X $210 X 8.5 mo. =	14,280		
		$29,410		
	Less adjustment for MBA = 6/20 X $29,410 =	−8,823		20,597
C.	Bookstore profits			N.A.
				$68,242

II. COSTS

A.	Library volumes (non-recurring) 300 X $20[3]		
	Continuing acquisitions		1,000
B.	Faculty		
	Salaries - 4 faculty $\frac{1}{4}$ time	$30,000	
	2 adjuncts	3,000	33,000

C.	Financial Aid: $\frac{1}{3}$ X Full-time tuition ($54,810)	18,270
D.	Facilities: Excess capacity - no addition to cost	N.A.
E.	GSH depreciation: Tenants pay damages	N.A.
F.	Professional meetings:	3,000
G.	Research	5,000
H.	Addition to MBA budget: Support	10,000
		−$70,270
	Incremental addition to revenue (deficit)	($2,028)

Assumptions and notes:

1. That 6 MBA students will defect to the MHCA, and that an overall increase in students would be 14, not 20.

2. That there will be 10 single students, 2 married students in furnished apartments, and 8 married students in unfurnished apartments.

3. Will be covered by a grant of $6,000. This cost is not included here.

The cost for 1980–81 has been:

Revenue

      Fall - 10 students at $135 hr. X 30 hours

      Spring - 17 students at $135 hr. X 30 hours

Although there is a small deficit in regard to revenue/cost analysis, the general thrust and benefit of the project seems to be favorable. Some of the benefits of the program cannot easily be assigned monetary value. Some of the more important benefits are:

1. Providing personnel for staffing requirements in the medical complex under construction.

2. Broadening the appeal of the MBA program.

3. Meeting the basic goals and purposes of Fairfield University to totally provide health care practitioners.

4. Meeting the needs of undergraduate students at Fairfield University for a quality HCA program in an environment conducive to their own goals and preferences.

CHAPTER V

CONCLUSIONS, RECOMMENDATIONS, AND LONG-RANGE PLAN

This study was conducted within the framework of the assumptions stated earlier. Based on the analysis of the Benefit/Cost considerations, the development of the Health-Care Administration is desirable. Although there is a minor increase in incremental cost because of the establishment of the program, the overriding long-term benefits listed in Chapter IV outweigh the less than breakeven situation.

The remainder of the conclusions and recommendations will be expressed in terms of a long-range plan to execute the recommendation of beginning the Health-Care Administration program at Fairfield University.

Long-Range Plan

The long-term plan described here was the sequence needed to start the instructional phase of the program by the fall term of 1981. This has been accomplished.

The first move was to appoint a temporary director to supervise the processes leading to offering the program. Dr. J. Charles Smith has taken that responsibility.

The second step was to encourage support for the program both within and outside the University community. That has been accomplished.

Step three was to establish liaison with the Schools of Business, Law, Dentistry, and Medicine. This was accomplished.

Step four was to recruit part-time faculty early in 1981 so that the health-care fields concerned can have an advisory role in curriculum planning. Drs. Capelli, Jones, and Ms. Johnson have been involved.

The fifth step now is to further develop the curriculum. Robert Williams is coordinating that this spring. This must be done in time to make brochures and catalog changes.

Step six is to recruit someone to teach Health Care IV.

Step seven should be library acquisitions, some 300 volumes. This should be completed by summer 1982.

The eighth step should be to begin screening applications for the next class in August 1982.

These preparations should be adequate to operate the program through its first year. In the spring of 1981, the ninth step should be taken— that of developing the internship program beginning in the summer of 1981. Robert Miller and Dr. Jones are taking responsibility for that.

Also at this time (1981) step number ten, that of completing negotiations to establish internships at various organizations and agencies, should be accomplished. Arrangements should also be completed with the University Medical Complex administration for placement in the hospital and clinics, and the University Retirement Nursing Care facilities.

In the summer of 1981, the first class should begin internships and the last objective of the developmental phase will have been accomplished. They will graduate with all other schools in May 1983.

APPENDIX A

CURRICULUM OUTLINE

Graduate Modular   12 hours

    Management

    Finance

    Accounting

    Marketing

    Research paper or thesis   6 hours

    Business Core   <u>27 hours</u>

                        Total   45 hours

SPECIAL ADDITIONAL CURRICULUM

A. <u>Introduction to Health-Care Administration</u> includes: 3 hours

    Definition of public health

    Structure of health-service organizations

    National Health Care policy

    Issues and problems in health care

    Personnel

B. HCA 5233 - <u>Health-Care Administration</u> includes   3 hours

    Principles of health-care administration, including

    Institutional and departmental services

    Health service management decision making

    Joint and Group Practices

C. HCA 5343 - <u>Health-Care Marketing</u> includes: 3 hours

    Marketing

    Health Needs

    Planning

D. Health Care Statistics includes: 3 hours

    Statistics and probability

    Mortality

    Morbidity

    Other health data

    Resource allocation and decision making

    Distribution problems

E. HCA 5453 - Policy and Health Planning includes: 3 hours

    Political considerations

    Strategic plan for HC organization

    Assessment of health needs and resources

    State and national health agencies

    Regional and local health departments

    Labor law in health care

    Social interface

    Computer games for decision making

    Case analysis

The student would complete the 45 hours over a 2-year, 4-semester program.

The degree plan sheet follows.

HEALTH CARE MANAGEMENT

DEGREE PLAN SHEET - 1981
TOTAL HRS REQ 45

NAME _____ Date _____

COURSES EARNED	COURSE CODE	COURSE TITLE	CR
		Semester I - Fall 1981	
	BUS 5723	Ethics of Gov, Bus & Soc	3
	MGT 5613	Mgt & Org Theory	3
	ACT 5623	Mgr Acc & Control	3
	MGT 5543H	Health Care Mgt I	3
	HPE 001*	Health Fitness I	.5
	PRF 0700	SWIMMING PROFICIENCY	
			12.5

COURSES EARNED	COURSE CODE	COURSE TITLE	CR
		Semester II - Spring 1982	
	BUS 5633	Financial Mgt	3
	MKT 5643	Marketing Mgt	3
	MGT 5543J	Health Care Mgt II	3
	MGT 5993A	Research I**	3
	HPE 002*	Health Fitness II	.5
			12.5

COURSES EARNED	COURSE CODE	COURSE TITLE	CR
		Semester III - Fall 1982	
	BUS 5823	Economic Theory	3
	MGT 5543KK	Health Care Stat	3
	MGT 5993B	Research II*	3
	HPE 026*	Beginning Swimming#	.5
			9.5

COURSES EARNED	COURSE CODE	COURSE TITLE	CR
		Semester IV - Spring 1983	
	BUS 5863	Quantitative Anal	3
	CPS 5772	Cross Pollination	2
	MGT 5543LL	Health Care Plan	3
	THE 5072	Holy Spirit	2
	HPE _____	Elective	.5
			10.5

#May be replaced by an HPE elective
if Swimming Proficiency has been passed

All students must pass proficiency exams in each of the following areas:

PRF 2020 Management   PRF 2000 Finance
PRF 2010 Accounting   PRF 2030 Marketing

**Research I & II must be completed in the Health Care Management Area.

	1st	2nd	3rd	4th	TOT REQ

√ - Reg completed ORU HRS EARNED _____

NA - Not applicable

E - Enrolled   TRANSFER HRS _____

S - Substituted

T - Transferred   TOTAL _____ = TOT EARN _____

TOTAL HOURS NEEDED _____

INDEX